To Katie
with love
Christmas 19 64

CHURCHILL

a pictorial biography

CHURCHILL
a pictorial biography

BY ALAN MOOREHEAD

 THAMES AND HUDSON · LONDON

CONTENTS

THE CHURCHILL FAMILY TREE

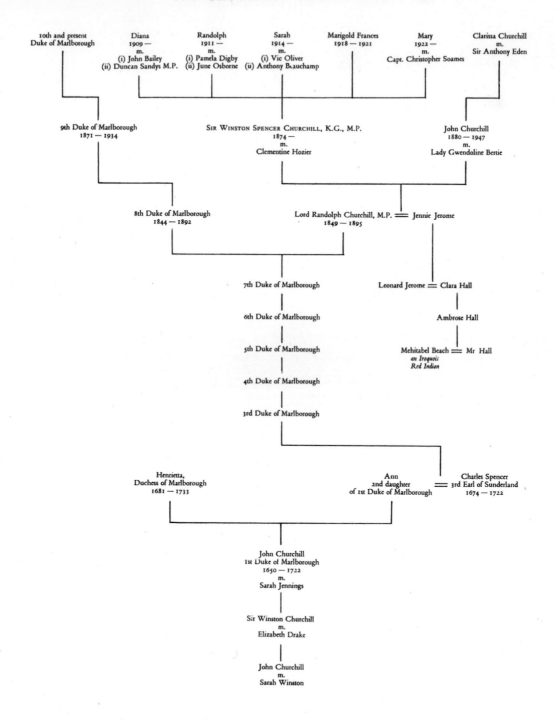

10th and present
Duke of Marlborough

Diana
1909 —
m.
(i) John Bailey
(ii) Duncan Sandys M.P.

Randolph
1911 —
m.
(i) Pamela Digby
(ii) June Osborne

Sarah
1914 —
m.
(i) Vic Oliver
(ii) Anthony Beauchamp

Marigold Frances
1918 — 1921

Mary
1922 —
m.
Capt. Christopher Soames

Clarissa Churchill
m.
Sir Anthony Eden

9th Duke of Marlborough
1871 — 1934

Sir Winston Spencer Churchill, K.G., M.P.
1874 —
m.
Clementine Hozier

John Churchill
1880 — 1947
m.
Lady Gwendoline Bertie

8th Duke of Marlborough
1844 — 1892

Lord Randolph Churchill, M.P. ══ Jennie Jerome
1849 — 1895

7th Duke of Marlborough

Leonard Jerome ══ Clara Hall

6th Duke of Marlborough

Ambrose Hall

5th Duke of Marlborough

Mehitabel Beach ══ Mr Hall
an Iroquois
Red Indian

4th Duke of Marlborough

3rd Duke of Marlborough

Henrietta,
Duchess of Marlborough
1681 — 1733

Ann
2nd daughter
of 1st Duke of Marlborough

Charles Spencer
══ 3rd Earl of Sunderland
1674 — 1722

John Churchill
1st Duke of Marlborough
1650 — 1722
m.
Sarah Jennings

Sir Winston Churchill
m.
Elizabeth Drake

John Churchill
m.
Sarah Winston

Blenheim Palace, near Woodstock, Oxford, Winston Churchill's birthplace, built by Sir John Vanbrugh for John Churchill, first Duke of Marlborough (1650–1722).

THE CRISES OF WINSTON CHURCHILL'S CAREER by which he is best known may not necessarily be the real crises of his life. In his youth his name became widely known in England because of his exploits in the Boer War; but the chances are that the zenith of his soldiering was reached two years earlier in the charge of the 21st Lancers at Omdurman, or even in some stray unheard-of incident at Sandhurst. As a young politician before the First World War he was notorious for his forthright imperialism, but it well might have been that his major experience in Parliament occurred on the day when, as a back-bencher of barely three months' standing, he rose and made a remarkable speech against rearmament in England. Then later, in 1915, his reputation became fixed unfairly in the failure of the Gallipoli campaign, and people with half-secret glee pointed to him as another case of the brilliant over-confident young man who had gone too far and too fast. But for Churchill himself the real setback at that time might not have been the collapse of the plan upon which he had set his heart, but his failure to move the crusted and stubborn conservatism of England personified in Admiral Fisher and Lord Kitchener.

And so it goes on through his thirties, forties and fifties; a succession of public acts which give his name a kind of stately flamboyance and surround him with controversy whatever he does; and always underneath the private struggle. It could have been that his fall from office in 1945 was more poignant to him than his rise to the emergency in the Battle of Britain, and the necessity to turn against the French fleet at Oran might have been a bitterer thing to accept than all the hostility he ever encountered in Russia.

Then beyond this—beyond these public and private crises—there remain those other commotions of an intensely personal and emotional nature which can never be really known or understood by anybody else. Who, for example, can say what Churchill's thoughts were on the birth of his third daughter, Marigold, at the very moment the bells were ringing for the victory in November 1918, and again at the death of that child three years later when he was endeavouring to stop a civil war in Ireland?

The birth of Winston Leonard Spencer Churchill, from *The Times* of 3 December 1874.

We have grown used to living with Churchill through many years, and he is as familiar to us as the headmaster at school or the captain of a ship on a long voyage. We know all about his painting, his brick-laying and his hats. But the inmost threads of his feelings can never have been perfectly revealed by his speeches, or by the myriad photographs, or even by his tears on the occasion of a victory or a celebration.

Still another thing intervenes. In the life of a living man who has continued to a great age and who remains persistently in the public eye it is the last lap that counts. We forget how he started the race and the uncertainties of the middle of the course. He is immured in the reputation of being a famous old man: it is the last ten or fifteen years that engage us, and it will not be until long after he has vanished from sight that anyone will see him young again: slim, agitated, anxious to do well, prone to endless misjudgments and accidents and not very respectable.

Nevertheless, if we are to have any real understanding of an exceptional man —especially so spontaneous an exception as Churchill in such an uncharted time as the last eighty years—we must go back to the beginnings, and try to walk beside him in another century; to live vicariously his life in its public and private aspects as though all these years were still lying in the future.

Churchill's parents: Lord Randolph Churchill (1849–1895), Chancellor of the Exchequer (1886), and Lady Randolph Churchill (1854–1922), *née* Jennie Jerome.

The story then must begin in the pleasant setting of Cowes Week in 1873. Mrs Leonard Jerome, an American living in Paris, had come over to England bringing her daughter Jennie with her. Lord Randolph Churchill, the third son of the seventh Duke of Marlborough, had arrived from Blenheim Palace; not the embattled old-young man who led the House of Commons in the eighties, but a youth of twenty-four on holiday. Jennie Jerome was nineteen and a great beauty. From all accounts their meeting at a ball on board the cruiser *Ariadne* was an idyllic thing. Within three days they were secretly engaged, and Lord Randolph was writing to his father, 'I love her better than life itself'. He went on, 'Mr Jerome is a gentleman who is obliged to live in New York to look after his business. I do not know what it is.'

Leonard Jerome in fact was a considerable personage, important in the financial and newspaper world and one of the men who established the sport of racing in America. He was not at all pleased when he learned that the Duke of Marlborough was objecting to the marriage on the grounds that it was too precipitate, and he withdrew his own consent. In the end, however, the marriage took place in the British Embassy in Paris on 15th April 1874. The following November Lady Randolph Churchill was staying at Blenheim with her husband when suddenly she was seized with the pains of childbirth. According

Childhood

9

With his mother, in 1876

At the age of 7, in 1881.

to one version she was out driving at the time; according to another she was attending a St Andrew's Day ball at the palace; but at all events there seems to have been only enough time to get her to a small cloakroom close to the front door, and Winston Churchill was born there a full six weeks before he was expected. The child was red-headed.

Most of the next eighteen years are a strange and cold story of unhappiness, or at any rate of maladjustment, in the midst of plenty. The child was directed into the accepted pattern of Victorian upper-class schooling, and he could make nothing of it. Lord Randolph very soon became swallowed up in politics, and the boy sometimes lost sight of him for months on end. His mother, meanwhile, was the adored but remote figure visiting the night nursery on the way to dinner. To a great extent, then, Winston's immediate affections became fixed upon his nanny, a Mrs Everest, and fixed with such devotion that in after years he took her picture with him wherever he went, and he always spoke of her with an emotion of simple and unaffected happiness.

But he was not permitted to be very long with Mrs Everest. At the age of seven he was sent to a boarding school in southern England, and although it may have seemed to others to have been a perfectly respectable place, Churchill hated it. In later years he remembered it only as an horrific Dickensian institution, where the boys were beaten until they screamed. For two years he languished at the bottom of his class, until finally his family realised that something was wrong and took him away. Then for three years he was at a school run by two ladies in Brighton, which was kinder but taught him very little. He contracted, at length, double pneumonia (the only malady that seems to have seriously troubled Churchill through his long life), and as a result it was decided that he should not be entered for Eton, which traditionally was the family school, but for Harrow, with its dry and invigorating position on the hill.

Harrow was not much of an improvement. He performed so appallingly in his entrance examination that one suspects he was accepted largely on the strength of his father's name. Latin and Greek were beyond him, and he remained among the dunderheads learning and relearning simple English long after his brighter contemporaries had gone on to higher classes. Although he did well at any sport like fencing and swimming where there was a practical object, he made no headway at all at cricket and football; nor was he very popular among his companions. None of this, however, seems to have seriously dampened his spirits; on the contrary, in the four and a half years he was at Harrow he developed an aggressive and even at times an arrogant spirit.

Upon just one count Churchill was an unusual boy. He developed quite soon an exceptional ease and confidence in the use of words, and this was coupled with an astonishing memory; he was even reputed to be able to reel off 1,200 lines of Macaulay's *Lays of Ancient Rome* from memory when he was not yet out of the lowest form. He was grateful to Harrow in later years for the grounding it gave him in the English language.

But it was quite another factor that settled his future. Despairing of his ever being able to make much headway in a learned profession, Lord Randolph remembered that the boy had always had a passion for toy soldiers—he had possessed no fewer than 1,500 of them in his nursery—and it was decided that he should be sent to Sandhurst. Here at least he ought to be able to qualify for an infantry cadetship. But even this was beyond the boy's abilities. He made two unsuccessful attempts to pass the entrance examination and then, after an intensive six months at a crammer's in the Cromwell Road in London, managed only to scrape into the cavalry, where the required standards were somewhat lower, chiefly because so few candidates could put up the money for horses and equipment. In the midst of this yet another

As a Harrow schoolboy, aged 15, in 1889.

The Old Fourth Form Room at Harrow: 'This interlude at school', Churchill wrote, 'makes a sombre grey patch upon the chart of my journey. It was an unending spell of worries.'

setback occurred: while playing with some companions in Lady Wimborne's garden at Bournemouth, Churchill leapt from a bridge on to a tree, missed his grip and fell thirty feet into a chine. He lay for three days unconscious, and then for three months in bed. 'For a year,' Churchill wrote later, 'I looked at life round a corner.' School he remembered as 'the only barren and unhappy period of my life'. He was now seventeen, and from the moment he had left Mrs Everest and the nursery practically nothing had gone well with him.

No one, not even Churchill himself, has fully explained the change that came over his life in this year 1892. Perhaps it was merely the release from the hateful restrictions of school, the vigour of the new life in the open air, the bands, the uniforms, the delayed effect of adolescence itself—or perhaps even a combination of all these things—but from now on everything which before was difficult becomes easy and delightful. It is almost as if his life had been quietly waiting, like a seed, for this special moment of fertility. He enjoys everything at Sandhurst, the early mornings on horseback, the manoeuvres, the staff dinners and the hunting. He goes up to London and gets himself involved in a music-hall brawl; on leave in his father's house in Connaught Place he meets the leading politicians of the day. And at the end of two years he passes out eighth out of his batch of 150.

Churchill, aged 19, with two brother officer cadets at Sandhurst, in 1894.

THE INSURRECTION IN CUBA.

LIEUTENANT CHURCHILL ON THE SPANISH OPERATIONS.

(CENTRAL NEWS TELEGRAM.)

NEW YORK, Saturday.—The *World*, with the object of placing the impartial opinions of a well-informed person before the public on the subject of the Spanish operations in Cuba, publishes a communication from Lieutenant Spencer Churchill, of the 14th Hussars, who recently greatly distinguished himself in the battle near Camaguay. This officer says that crossing the boundary of Puerto Principe in the search for Maceo along most difficult routes, the ways being flooded and the heat almost insupportable and skirmishing constantly happening, the Spanish encountered Gomez and Maceo on December 2nd near the Reforma plantation. An important battle was fought. The field of battle was open, and extended about half a mile, being flanked by forests, while the enemy was hidden in fields overgrown with underwood, their rearguard being on the edge of a forest. The Spanish infantry advanced calmly to within thirty yards of the strong position to which the enemy's wings had been driven in and then charging, carried it. Of the Spaniards General Suarez Valdes, who, riding a white horse, marshalled the infantry, presented an excellent mark for the enemy's bullets. General Navarro, who commissioned the advance guard, skilfully handled his men on the rising ground, and the insurgents firing badly sent their hail of bullets over the heads of the staff where he (the lieutenant) was. The losses of the Spaniards would have been far heavier if the aim of the rebels had been better, because the troops were marching in close order on an open stretch of country towards formidable protected positions. Lieutenant Churchill says he felt extremely impressed in observing the valour and even the unconcern of the Spanish troops. They laughed and sang under a sustained fire, and their perfect discipline was alone comparable to that of the Roman soldiery. The troops subsequently returned to Cienfuegos. In conclusion, Lieutenant Churchill asserts that the methods of warfare in vogue among European armies are impracticable in Cuba.

MADRID, Saturday.—A Havana despatch to the *Imparcial* says that the military Red Cross has been accorded to Lieutenants Spencer Churchill and Barnes for gallant behaviour at the recent victory gained by General Suarez Valdes.

From the London *Daily Graphic* of 9 December 1895, reporting an interview with Lieutenant Churchill on his arrival in New York from the Cuban War. His first despatches as a war correspondent appeared anonymously in the *Daily Graphic*.

Soon after he was posted from Sandhurst to the 4th Hussars. He managed to get permission to visit the Spanish expeditionary forces which were struggling against a rebellion in Cuba, and with a young companion from his regiment he sailed for New York and Havana. On his twenty-first birthday, 30th November 1896, he came under hostile rifle fire for the first time in the jungle outside Arroyo Blanco. In his English uniform he sat his horse very straightly as the bullets went past, and that was one more stage that was passed on the journey to find himself. At that time very few young British officers had been under fire, and he returned, elatedly, one imagines, to an agreeable six months' vacation in England. Then in the autumn he sailed with his regiment for India.

It is perhaps still possible in the nineteen-sixties to understand something of the spaciousness and the security of the great houses of Victorian England, and the lives of privileged young men like Churchill, who moved in a small circle between Westminster and the hunting field, knowing everyone who mattered, having some relative or acquaintance in every high office. But the satellite offshoot of this world which was the Indian Army had an atmosphere that is more difficult to recapture, and even Kipling was an outsider looking in. It had a tradition that was half Pompeian and half public school, and for a young cavalry officer it had delights that will not easily be known again. He had his bungalow and his string of polo ponies, his butler, his dressing-boys and his syce. He had a family allowance of £400 or £500 a year above his pay, and if this did not suffice there were always the native money-lenders in the village.

In a really enthusiastic regiment polo was played, not as a game, but as the object of life itself, and all other occasions, even the day's work, were simply an interruption to the training for the inevitable inter-regimental competition that lay ahead.

The interesting thing about Churchill is not that he should have taken to this life at once and

The Royal Military College, Sandhurst, in 1881.

succeeded in it so well (he was one of the best horsemen in his regiment), but that, loving it so much, he should have begun so soon to turn away from it. The Hussars were stationed at Bangalore, three thousand feet above sea level, and in the calm and settled south of India; and after a few months Churchill grew restless. Fighting was going on along the north-west frontier, 2,000 miles away, and he managed to get himself posted there just in time to take part in a heavy skirmish with the tribesmen. Honour and glory were the things, and he was determined to have them.

All this perhaps was no break with the known pattern of his life up till then, but presently something much more important happened; at the age of twenty-two he began for the first time in his life to take to serious reading. The impact of these studies altered the course of his life; now for the first time he really began to outdistance his contemporaries. He read in the way that only an empty hungry mind can do when there is no specific object or examination in view but simply an overmastering absorption in the subject; and after so many arid intellectual years he was able to learn, no doubt, at a tremendous rate. Through the four or five hot hours of the day at Bangalore, when his companions were sleeping or playing whist, he read first Gibbon and Macaulay and then advanced amain upon Schopenhauer, Darwin, Plato and Aristotle. The inevitable reactions

Officer and War Correspondent

Churchill, aged 21, wearing the full-dress uniform of a subaltern in the 4th Queen's Own Hussars.

THE STORY

OF THE

MALAKAND FIELD FORCE

AN EPISODE OF FRONTIER WAR

BY

WINSTON L. SPENCER CHURCHILL

Lieutenant, the 4th Queen's Own Hussars

" They (Frontier Wars) are but the surf that marks the edge and the advance of the wave of civilisation."

LORD SALISBURY, Guildhall, 1892

WITH MAPS, PLANS, ETC.

LONGMANS, GREEN, AND CO.

39 PATERNOSTER ROW, LONDON

NEW YORK AND BOMBAY

1898

'I resolved to build a small literary house.' Churchill's first book, written at Bangalore, India, when he was 23.

followed—regret at the lack of a university training, resentment that he should have been so limited and even misled by his teaching at school, and finally, under the influence of such works as Winwood Reade's *Martyrdom of Man*, the first misgivings about religion. For a time he passed through 'a violent and aggressive anti-religious phase', which was corrected, he says, in later days by frequent contact with physical danger. He arrived then at a solution which, as Miss Virginia Cowles says in her study of Churchill, was almost feminine: he would believe what he wanted

I have not insulted the British public, by writing a party pamphlet, on a great Imperial question. I have recorded the facts as they occurred, and the impressions as they arose, without attempting to make a case against any person or any policy. Indeed, I fear that assailing none, I may have offended all. Neutrality may degenerate into an igno-minious isolation. An honest and unpre-judiced attempt to discern the truth, is my sole defence, as the good opinion of the reader has been throughout my chief aspira-tion, and can be in the end my only support.

WINSTON L. S. CHURCHILL,
Lieutenant, the 4th Queen's Own Hussars.

CAVALRY BARRACKS,
BANGALORE, *30th December,* 1897.

SAVROLA

A TALE OF THE REVOLUTION IN LAURANIA

BY

WINSTON SPENCER CHURCHILL
AUTHOR OF "THE RIVER WAR: AN HISTORICAL ACCOUNT OF THE RECONQUEST OF THE SOUDAN," ETC.

LONGMANS, GREEN, AND CO.
39 PATERNOSTER ROW, LONDON
NEW YORK AND BOMBAY
1900

From the Preface to the *Malakand Field Force*: a glimpse of the future war historian.

Churchill's only novel, written in 1898: 'I have consistently urged my friends to abstain from reading it.'

to believe. *Le cœur a ses raisons, que la raison ne connaît pas.* With this Churchill appears to have continued to the present day.

Meanwhile his own writing had begun. When he was with the north-west frontier forces he had sent back a series of dispatches which were published in the *Pioneer* of Allahabad and the London *Daily Telegraph*, and these he now reshaped into his first book, *Story of the Malakand Field Force*. It was published in 1898. Then in the space of two months, under the eye of his brother officers, he rattled off *Savrola*, his first and only novel, which was set in a Ruritanian republic and contained as a climax an account of a battle fleet forcing its way through a sort of straits not unlike the Dardanelles. One glance at either of these two productions makes it clear that underneath the borrowed style a professional writer was at work. The war dispatches were widely praised, and *Savrola*, at first serialised in *Macmillan's Magazine* and then published as a book in 1900,

The charge of the 21st Lancers, on 2 September 1898. 'For the first time that morning', Churchill wrote, 'I experienced a sudden sensation of fear. I thought these riflemen would hit me and the rest devour me like wolves. . . .'

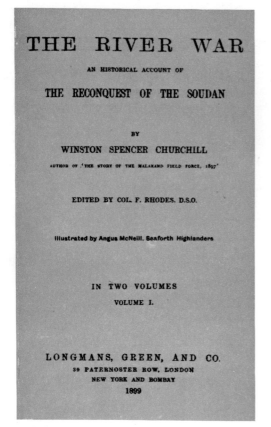

THE RIVER WAR

AN HISTORICAL ACCOUNT OF

THE RECONQUEST OF THE SOUDAN

BY

WINSTON SPENCER CHURCHILL

AUTHOR OF 'THE STORY OF THE MALAKAND FIELD FORCE, 1897'

EDITED BY COL. F. RHODES. D.S.O.

Illustrated by Angus McNeill, Seaforth Highlanders

IN TWO VOLUMES

VOLUME I.

LONGMANS, GREEN, AND CO.
39 PATERNOSTER ROW, LONDON
NEW YORK AND BOMBAY
1899

The River War, Churchill's third book, appeared in 1899. Its outspoken criticism of Kitchener caused a sensation in military circles.

brought in the surprisingly large sum of seven hundred pounds.

In 1897 Churchill had three very active years of soldiering ahead of him—the years which were to turn him from a private into a public figure and make his name famous throughout the world. General Sir Herbert Kitchener was in Egypt, mounting an expedition that was to proceed up the Nile Valley and avenge the death of General Gordon by attacking the Khalifah in the Sudan. Directly Churchill heard of these plans it was intolerable to him that he should remain in a quiet regimental life in India. Returning on leave to England, he used every influence that was open to him in Whitehall to get himself attached to the expedition.

But this time there were difficulties. His *Story of the Malakand Field Force* had contained certain criticisms of the high command, and the generals not unreasonably disliked it. In the end, however, Churchill found a friend in Sir Evelyn Wood, the Adjutant General, and a place was made for him in the 21st Lancers. Before he left London for Cairo he made arrangements with the *Morning Post* to supply a series of dispatches at £15 a column.

The Sudan campaign was a model of what is now known as the science of logistics (or supply), and the terrible setpiece battle outside Omdurman in which the dervishes were defeated was colonial warfare on the grand scale. But it has always been overshadowed in public memory by one incident in the battle—the charge of the 21st Lancers. This was the last of the classic cavalry charges before the machine-gun took control, the last flourish of the panoply of nineteenth century warfare in the tradition of the Light Brigade in the Crimea and the troopers at Waterloo. As a military operation it could scarcely be accounted an unqualified success. Some three hundred horsemen took part, launching themselves and their lances at full gallop upon a mass of several thousand dervishes, and it was all over in three minutes. When the British retired it was found that nearly a quarter of their number had been cut down, and 120 horses destroyed, while but forty or fifty dervishes lay on the ground. Yet even today it is impossible to visit Omdurman without feeling something of the stir and the excitement of that gallop. Churchill was just twenty-four at the time, and he was in the thick of it. He was unable to hold a lance because he had dislocated his shoulder, but he carried a pistol, and finding himself alone among the dervishes at the end of the charge he somehow managed to shoot his way back into the British lines. Young Lieutenant Beatty of the Royal Navy (who had tossed a bottle of champagne ashore to him the night before), was watching quietly from a gunboat on the Nile close by.

On his way back to England Churchill fell in with G. W. Steevens, the war correspondent of the London *Daily Mail,* and Steevens was captivated by him. He seems to have seen more clearly than anyone else up to this time that the young cavalry officer was someone quite exceptional in the world. An article appeared in the *Daily Mail* entitled 'the Youngest Man in Europe'. In it Steevens committed himself to some unusual and reckless phrases, predicting that Churchill might become 'a great popular leader, a great journalist or the founder of a great advertising business'.

Churchill himself does not seem to have been altogether unaware of these stirrings. His adventures at Omdurman brought him to a series of clear decisions. First, he must get out of the army and into a wider life. Second, he must make money—and the obvious way to do this was by writing. And third, he would follow his father into politics. Even now, half a century away, one feels a certain sense of awe at the complete determination with which, against every obstacle, he accomplished all these things within the space of the next two years. No move is wasted, nothing diverts him from this final leap out of youth into fame.

First he returned to the Army in India with the express object of rounding off his career as a polo player by taking part in the inter-regimental competition at Meerut, an event he accomplished very satisfactorily by hitting three of the winning goals in the final match despite the fact that his dislocated shoulder was strapped up to his side. Then having completed *The River War,* his splendid account of the Sudan campaign, he resigned from the Army and fought his first election as a Tory at Oldham. Here he was defeated by the future Lord Runciman and the Liberal Party, but he appears to have wasted no time in regrets.

Almost at once, in October 1899, he set off for the Boer War, travelling aboard the *Dunottar Castle* with General Buller and his staff as a civilian war correspondent. Even by present standards the arrangements he made with the *Morning Post* were exceptionally good: he was to have £250 a month and all his expenses paid.

As wars go, the Boer War is something of an anachronism: it bears a much

A group of famous war correspondents in the South African War, 1899, with Churchill, then just 25, seated, second from the left.

closer resemblance to some of the early African and Middle East campaigns in 1940 and 1941 than to anything that happened in the First World War. There was the same space for manoeuvre across the empty land, the quick tactical changes, the sieges, the emphasis on the individual, and above all the feeling that this was not so much an all-out struggle for the existence of civilisation itself but, rather, a desperate professional game fought out in the open with its own special rules and conditions. This was an atmosphere that suited Church-ill's temperament perfectly; he was not tied to the trenches and the headquarters of a set-piece battle, he could move around. One feels he would have behaved in exactly the same way forty years later at the siege of Tobruk and in the long marches across the desert from El Alamein.

Within a fortnight of arriving at Capetown he was captured by the Boers. Within a month he has escaped from Pretoria into Portuguese East Africa. And within a year, having attended nearly all the major actions, he was triumphantly back in England.

It is a remarkable story of courage and the utmost energy, and the most re-markable part of all was his escape. In the last few years we have been sated with gallant escape stories of every possible kind, but very few of them, either in their literary quality or in their excitement, can compare with Churchill's

SECOND EDITION.

MORNING POST, Nov. 17. 6.25 A.M.

THE TRANSVAAL WAR.

ARMOURED TRAIN TRAPPED.

MR. CHURCHILL CAPTURED.

HIS COOLNESS AND BRAVERY.

FURTHER DETAILS.

COLENSO RAILWAY CUT.

LADYSMITH FIGHTING

BOERS DEFEATED.

FROM OUR WAR CORRESPONDENT.

DURBAN, Nov. 15, 10.25 A.M.

Churchill was captured by the Boers on 15 November 1899 when accompanying an armoured reconnaissance train. He escaped from Pretoria Prison four weeks later.

own account of his adventures on the African veldt. He climbs the prison wall when the sentry's back is turned, he walks boldly down the centre of the road through the enemy capital, he leaps on to the first moving train he sees and by a special providence it carries him in the right direction. Fearing that he will be discovered he leaves the train in the morning and wanders about, still hundreds of miles behind the enemy's lines, until at last, made desperate by hunger and despair, he gives himself up to the one man in the whole countryside who, it happens, is English and willing to help him.

The Boers naturally are on the lookout for him on every road and railway and in every kraal. A reward of £25 is offered for the capture, dead or alive, of Winston Churchill, 'Englishman, 25 years old, about five feet eight inches tall, indifferent build, walks with a forward stoop, pale appearance, red-brownish hair, small and hardly noticeable moustache, talks through his nose and cannot pronounce the letter "s" properly.'

Meanwhile Churchill lies low in the disused gallery of a coal mine reading Stevenson's *Kidnapped*. There is a particularly unpleasant episode with white rats in the darkness of the mine before he finally gets away.

This story made a sensation in England. The war then was going badly, and public imagination was in need of a hero. It seized on Churchill, and when instead of coming home at once he continued to send a stream of absorbing dispatches to the *Morning Post* from the most dangerous places, his reputation grew rather than diminished.

Since his experience included such exploits as riding on a bicycle through Johannesburg while the city was still in the hands of the Boers, it was astonishing that he was never hit or even so much as scraped by a bullet. His younger brother John was wounded, and very many others who exposed themselves far less than Churchill survived only a short time on the veldt. It was not unnatural then that somewhere about this time, having seen more fighting than almost any

The Boer War 1899–1902; a street in a prisoner-of-war camp. 'Here the hours crawled like paralytic centipedes,' Churchill wrote.

other Englishman of his own age, he began to conceive the idea that some special destiny was awaiting him: he had only to continue boldly and all would be well.

When finally on the fall of Pretoria he came home to contest the khaki election of 1900, he was approached by the Conservatives in eleven different constituencies. He chose, however, to go back to Oldham, and Oldham, with the bands playing, hung itself with banners: 'The Conquering Hero'.

He emerged with a majority of 222 votes.

There were still some months to go before he took his seat in this last of Queen Victoria's Parliaments, and he set off on a lecture tour through England. The proceeds of this tour (he was paid £300 for a single lecture at Liverpool), together with his earnings from his books and the *Morning Post*, brought him in a sum of about £4,500.

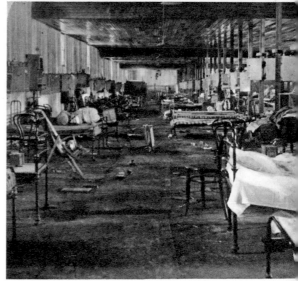

Stud Hall', the last prison occupied by the British officers in Pretoria.

Queen Victoria in 1899.

Then, crossing to New York, he earned a further £10,000 on a tour through the United States. Mark Twain was one of his chairmen. British income tax at the time was one shilling in the pound.

When at last in January 1901 he came down to the House of Commons to take his father's old seat on the back benches, every one of the objects he had set himself had been completed. He was famous, he was an established writer, he was comfortably off, he was in the House at last, and moreover, against all the odds, he was alive. Alive and aged just twenty-six.

Upon all the evidence the year 1900 ought to have been something of a landmark in English history. No sooner was the general election over than Queen Victoria fell ill, and when in the following January she died it seemed for a time that this was an uprooting change in everybody's life, and that with the new century a new era had begun.

Yet nothing really happened. The vast accumulated mass of Victorian habits and traditions kept rolling on, and people either would not or could not change. On and off through twenty years the Conservatives had dominated politics, and the Cecils had dominated the Conservatives; and now Lord Salisbury was back in power again, with the Liberals as usual in opposition. The Boer War dragged wretchedly on, but Britain was still incontestably the greatest power in the world. Of Adolf Hitler, a schoolboy in Austria, of Mussolini, an impoverished school-teacher in Italy, and of Stalin, who had just been expelled from a theological college in Tiflis for political activities, not the slightest whisper had yet been heard. Income tax went down to elevenpence in the pound and the Labour Party was nothing.

Conservative Member of Parliament

In these circumstances Winston Churchill got up after dinner on 18th February 1901 and made his first speech in Parliament. As maiden speeches go it was something out of the usual run. He was already well known because of his books and his South African exploits, and members were naturally interested to see how Lord Randolph's son would acquit himself. They were not disappointed. The speech was prepared in the same way as Churchill's chief speeches have been prepared ever since—that is to say, it was written out beforehand, and on this occasion he learned it off by heart. It was brief, it dealt with the burning question of the moment—the conduct of the war—it steered a neat

Member of Parliament for Oldham, 1901, aged 26.

course between the hard-war policy of the Conservatives and the pro-Boer sympathies of the Liberals, and it wound up with a graceful reference to his father.

Not a bombshell of a speech but good enough for *Punch* to comment that he had his father's 'command of pointed phrase', and for Mr Chamberlain—'Old Joe', who was the commanding figure on the Treasury benches—to say that they might well see 'the father repeated in the son'.

This really was the point, and because it was such an obvious thing to say very few people, certainly not Old Joe himself, realised its significance at the time.

It is a notable thing in Churchill's life that at each stage of his career he appears always to have fixed upon some central compelling object.

In 1901 his first rage for physical action had expended itself—indeed, another fifteen years were to go by before he returned to active soldiering—and he was filled with an entirely different ambition. This, quite simply, was to re-create and vindicate his father's political life.

Churchill had never really known his father, or at any rate he had never known him as intimately as he had wished to do. Always at those moments when they might have talked the boy was away at school or with the Army. More and more, until his illness gained on him, Lord Randolph was immersed in his own career. He remained to his son an awesome figure, splendid, incorruptible, wrongfully abused, and remote.

In June 1894 Lord Randolph set out on a journey round the world in a last hopeless attempt to restore his health, and Churchill came up to London to see him off. 'His face looked terribly haggard and worn with mental pain. He patted me on the knee in a gesture which however simple was perfectly informing . . . I never saw him again, except as a swiftly fading shadow.' Lord Randolph came home to die the following year at the age of forty-five.

Now, six years later, Churchill was possessed by these memories. He set up his father's old desk and chair in his study, dipped his pen in his father's brass inkpot and hung his father's picture on the wall before him. One after another he sought out his father's friends, learning and re-learning his father's policies; and presently he launched himself upon a major work, a full-length biography of Lord Randolph's stormy life. And while this mental image was being steadily built up, month by month, in the privacy of his rooms, he proceeded in public to re-create his father in the flesh. Lord Randolph's enemies would be his enemies. Lord Randolph had been a rebel and he would be one too. In the House members began to see the father's gestures and mannerisms consciously repeated when the son got up to speak; and the words he uttered contained the same measured defiance.

Earl Winterton, who had as good an opportunity as anyone for observing Churchill at this time, has said that he was not popular in the House. He was too aggressive, too eager to hunt down his father's old enemies, and, as it was thought at the time, far too ambitious. It was not until later, when he had

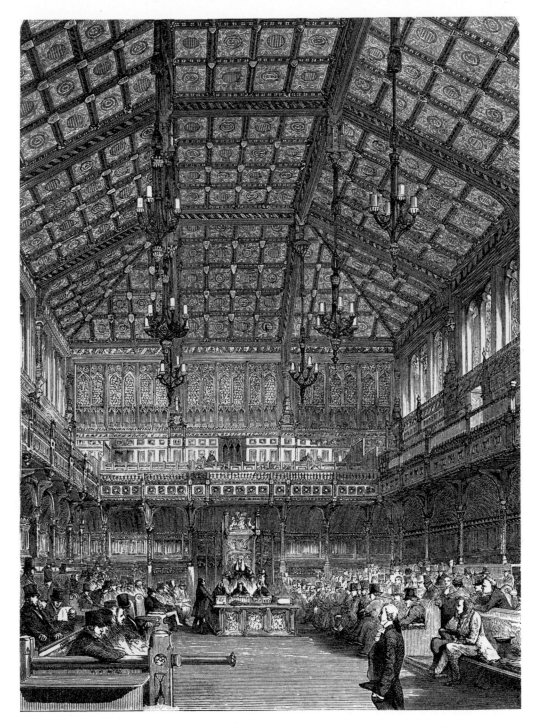

The House of Commons in the early days of Queen Victoria.

achieved a happy marriage and high office, that he mellowed and the House began to expand towards him.

But in the early nineteen-hundreds there was no question of promoting Churchill to office. He spoke on the average once or twice a month, sniping persistently at the unfortunate Brodrick, constantly leading a small group of rebels against the accepted party line. The final break came in 1903. Joseph Chamberlain, as Minister for the Colonies, was determined upon the abandon- ment of Free Trade, and this to Churchill, brought up all his life in the atmosphere of laissez-faire, was anathema. Free Trade to the Churchills—and to many other Conservatives as well—was more than a policy: it was almost an article of faith. He embarked on a full-scale attack on the government, and when the House rose for recess continued his personal campaign on Chamberlain all through the summer. It was remembered now that Chamberlain had been one of the chief opponents of his father.

Despite this it might still have been possible for the Tories to have found a place for Churchill in the reshuffle of Cabinet which was occasioned by this issue, but Mr Balfour had succeeded Lord Salisbury as Prime Minister, and he was not in a forgiving mood. When the House reassembled in 1904, Churchill became the centre of a series of scenes of extreme bitterness. Once he was shouted down by his own party. On another occasion Balfour and almost all the Conservatives walked out when he got up to speak. At Oldham his own electors disowned him. Clearly this false position could continue no longer, and in May 1904, amid the contempt and derision of the Conservatives, Churchill crossed the House to the Liberal side.

In the election that followed two years later the Liberals came in on a land- slide with 401 seats against 157, and Churchill was even less endeared to the defeated Conservatives when it was learned that his new friends had given him the post of Under Secretary for the Colonies. Now finally, it was said, the truth was out: here was the renegade who changed his party to obtain office, the political adventurer who would do anything for his own advancement. 'He was,' it was said, 'the most hated man in the House of Commons.'

It is a curious and arresting aspect of Churchill's story that for a man who has been more constantly in the public eye than perhaps any other individual in the present century so little importance should be attached to his private life. It seems to flow on in a calm backwater of its own. At no point does it impinge on his public career. No matter how tumultuous the public scene, everything here appears to remain serene, well ordered and detached. No breath of scandal ever touches it. The doubts, the self-questionings and the occasional back- slidings that bedevil most men at some time or another in the private passages of their lives appear to have no place with Churchill at all. He is not a visionary or a missionary or a poet; one thinks of him rather as a sober contemporary tramping along at the head of history. His world is here and now and he is very clear about his direction.

Joseph Chamberlain (1836–1914), Colonial Secretary (1895–1903), friend of both Churchill and his father.

Arthur J. Balfour (1848–1930), succeeded Churchill's father in 1886, and Churchill himself in 1915.

It might well be, of course, that Churchill's personality is a sort of inverted iceberg, with eight-ninths showing above the surface and only one-ninth below. But even the submerged ninth has been thoroughly displayed. Except for the really deep sources of his thoughts one feels one knows it all just as well as the private life of a public man will ever be known. A 'character' has been built up, a kind of Rowlandson patriot-hero, and the net effect may have made us overlook the only thing that really counts, and that is the remarkable solidity of this life, the enormous strength he has gained from his family and his traditions. He makes all his forays out into the world from a sure base at home. Politics are not for him a matter of personal life or death or of revolutionary causes; they are something added to life, a technique, a means for a man to express his talents and beliefs in the most responsible way, and even sometimes no more than a game. It was this view, as we shall see later, that involved him in the sharpest disappointments and conflicts of his career.

It was through these years, from 1906 onwards, when outwardly his fortunes

Winston Churchill and his fiancée, Clementine Hozier, at the time of their engagement.

seemed most controversial, that Churchill began to arrange his private life, to pad it out and make it comfortable for the journey ahead in the most sensible and practical way. When he was still only thirty he published his life of Lord Randolph, and even his opponents could hardly refrain from applause. It was a masterful arrangement of the facts, beautifully and movingly written, and was everywhere reviewed with enthusiasm. With his savings and his income from this and his other books he still had ample means to live a bachelor's life. At this time he shared a flat in Mayfair with his brother John, and even then, according to his friends, he kept a good table and an interesting wardrobe. He worked incessantly. The time other men spend in gambling or in entertainment and society he devoted to the House, to the polishing of his speeches (sometimes as much as six weeks' work on a single speech), and to reading. If one excepts an occasional game of polo, he had at this stage no hobbies; he was beset with a sense of urgency, a feeling that there was not much time left, that he might die in his forties as his father had done before him.

Marriage   It was while he was fighting a by-election in Scotland in 1908 that he met Clementine Hozier, and soon afterwards he proposed to her when they were out walking in the grounds of Blenheim Palace. It was an attachment that was suitable in every possible way. She was a daughter of Colonel Sir Henry Hozier and Lady Blanche Hozier, and a grand-daughter of the Countess of Airlie, a strong supporter of the Liberal cause. Clementine Hozier was a beautiful girl, aged twenty-three, eleven years younger than Churchill. She had finished her education at the Sorbonne in Paris, and was herself interested in politics. Her family was not wealthy, and it was evident from the beginning that the couple would have to make their way together. Their marriage in St Margaret's, Westminster, was one of the social events of the 1908 season, and for this moment, at least, there was a pause in the political hostility of the Tories; Lord Hugh Cecil was the best man, and presents arrived from Arthur Balfour and the Chamberlains. Their first child, Diana (the wife of Duncan Sandys, the present Minister of Aviation), was born the following year, and there followed Randolph (1911), Sarah (1914), who early in her career on the stage married the actor Vic Oliver, Marigold (1918), who died as a small child, and Mary (1922), who married Christopher Soames, Churchill's parliamentary private secretary until the time of his retirement as Prime Minister.

The early years of the marriage cannot have been particularly easy for Mrs Churchill. Although from time to time Churchill visited his cousin the Duke of Marlborough at Blenheim, most of the other Tory houses were closed to him. He was openly regarded as a 'traitor to his own class', and it was felt that he should stew in his own juice among the cranks and radicals of the Liberal Left. Nevertheless, there were plenty of other friends who were very ready to welcome the Churchills, and it is against the background of a thriving and more than usually united family that one has to consider the next nine years that carried him in a crescendo of publicity to the first of the two great heights of his career.

As Under Secretary for the Colonies Chur-

The Times for Monday, 14 September 1908: part of a two-column description of Churchill's wedding.

MR. CHURCHILL'S WEDDING.

THE SCENE AT ST. MARGARET'S.

The wedding of Mr. Churchill, M.P., President of the Board of Trade, and Miss Clementine Hozier at St. Margaret's, Westminster, on Saturday, undoubtedly captured the public imagination. This was shown not only by the crowded state of the church during the ceremony, but by the remarkable scene which was witnessed outside. Great numbers of well-dressed people lined all the roadways leading to St. Margaret's, and waited with the utmost patience to see the wedding party and the guests arrive and drive away again. The police were present in considerable force, mounted and on foot, and their services were quite necessary to marshal the crowds and to preserve clear the approaches to the church. That the people were animated by kindlier feelings than mere curiosity was made manifest by their cheers. Both the bride and bridegroom were cordially cheered as they came to the church, and when they emerged from the north porch after the ceremony and drove away in their motor-car to Portland-place they were greeted with an enthusiasm that is rarely displayed even at weddings at St. Margaret's.

Within the church political opponents joined with friends and colleagues in expressing their good will towards the President of the Board of Trade and his bride. Many of the guests had travelled long distances in order to be present. The accommodation of St. Margaret's, indeed, was taxed to its utmost capacity to contain the guests, and long before the hour for the wedding arrived the church was filled. The time of waiting afforded ample opportunity to note and appreciate the exquisite setting which had been prepared for the marriage ceremony. The chancel was decked with a profusion of white flowers, their beauty emphasized by plants and creepers of green. On the altar, within the communion rails, along the choir stalls, and about the chancel steps were masses of white chrysanthemums, lilies, and feathery spiræa. In effective contrast with these were the towering palms and the heaped up banks of ferns, smilax, maidenhair, and other creeping growths. Through the stained glass windows the sunshine streamed full upon the flowers, and touched with sudden brightness the beautiful reredos and the carved woodwork of the choir stalls. There were more flowers and palms at the north porch to greet the coming of the bride. The remainder of the church had been left unadorned.

While the strains of the March from *Tannhäuser* pealed forth from the organ the seats in the nave, which had been reserved for the relations and intimate friends of the bride and bridegroom, rapidly filled. Lady Blanche Hozier, the mother of the bride, who wore a gown of purple silk, was escorted to her seat by Lord Redesdale. Her mother, the Dowager Countess of Airlie, a venerable figure in black, was an early arrival. Lady St. Helier was also in black, with black and silver bonnet and scarf. With her came Lady Charles Beresford in a biscuit-colour costume. Near them were Lady Stanley of Alderley and Miss Stanley. Lady Maude Whyte, an aunt of the bride's, wore a black and white striped silk gown. Mrs. George Cornwallis West, Mr. Churchill's mother, in a dark mushroom coloured gown, with large hat trimmed with dahlias, occupied a seat close to the chancel steps. With her were Mrs. Moreton Frewen, Mrs. John Leslie, Lady Wimborne, and other members of the bridegroom's family.

chill had the job of putting through a bill that was very much to his liking: the granting of self-government to the Transvaal and the Orange Free State. This was an immediate success, and was the start of the close relations which Churchill has maintained with South Africa ever since. With the passage of this bill he moved very quickly into the top ranks of the Liberal Party, and when Asquith took over the Prime Ministership from Campbell-Bannerman in 1908 he was given the Board of Trade with a seat in the Cabinet. His companions now were Grey at the Foreign Office, Haldane, who was engaged in over-hauling the Army, John Morley at the India Office, Asquith himself, and, most important of all, Lloyd George, who was Chancellor of the Exchequer.

The Liberal Minister The association of Churchill and Lloyd George seems to have sprung from an immediate recognition of ability on either side, for there was precious little similarity in their background, their training or their personalities. From this point onwards the two men go careering through British politics together as though they had an instinctive knowledge that they were destined for the top; Lloyd George in his trilby, Churchill in his frock coat, the one man supple, intricate and irreverent, the other pugnacious, formalistic, and impulsive; and it is Lloyd George, by eleven years the senior, who is the master and Churchill the willing pupil. Within the next few years these two became the most forceful speakers in the House, and the most controversial figures in the country.

Lloyd George undoubtedly did more than anyone else to bring Liberal prin-ciples to life in Churchill's mind, to stimulate him and reveal the horizons that lay ahead; more important still, it was through the same source that Churchill about this time began to discover the working class.

As a young man Churchill had regarded the poor through very blue spec-tacles indeed. In the 4th Hussars he and his brother officers had strongly agreed upon the value of the Christian religion for the lower orders—'Nothing can give them a good time here, but it makes them more contented to think that they will get one hereafter.' Later as a young candidate for election he was able to remark rather grandly: 'I like the British working man, and so did my father before me.' Nor was his handling of the suffragettes much more subtle. They were not mollified with his eager 'Trust *me,* ladies'; they continued to heckle him ruthlessly on the platform and were even instrumental in bringing him down in one by-election.

But now, under Lloyd George's tutelage and out of his own awakened inter-est in the workers' conditions, he was aflame to put things to rights; and at the Board of Trade he had the means at his disposal. Churchill's part in the social legislation between 1908 and 1911 was soon forgotten in the First World War, and finally obliterated from his enemies' memory in the bitterness of the general strike fifteen years later, but it was sincere and it was important. Old-age pen-sions, sickness insurance, labour exchanges and impartial trade boards which fixed fairer rates of pay and hours of work—in the establishment of all these Churchill took a hand, and the speeches he made at the time would have

Budget Day, 1910: David Lloyd George, Chancellor of the Exchequer, and Winston Churchill, Home Secretary, on their way to the House of Commons.

caused no uneasiness in the Labour Party now.

But the central issue of the day—the issue, in fact, which at last awoke the country to the twentieth century and the coming era of the mass-produced man—was the Lloyd George budget of 1909. It was not, in the amount of money involved, a sensational budget, but it was aimed squarely at the rich, and presently Lloyd George and Churchill between them, perhaps with a view to bringing things to a crisis, began to increase their attacks upon the upper classes with a series of provocative speeches.

For some time previous to this the House of Lords (pleasantly described by Lloyd George as 'Mr Balfour's poodle'), had been rejecting or drastically amending many of the Liberal bills. Now they threw out this budget, and matters came to a head. Two general elections fought in 1910 in circumstances of great rancour made it perfectly clear that the Liberals could not be turned out, and

Herbert Henry Asquith (1858-1928). 'His opinions in the prime of his life were cut in bronze.'

'Votes for Women!' A suffragette demonstration in front of Buckingham Palace.

The First Lord of the Admiralty, addressing a meeting in February 1912.

Richard Burdon Haldane (1856–1928), War Minister 1906–1915, the creator of the modern British Army.

Asquith felt strong enough to show his hand. He informed Balfour, the leader of the Tory Opposition, that he was prepared, with the King's consent, to swamp the Upper House by the creation of 400 new liberal-minded peers; and at this the Lords capitulated. A bill went through limiting their powers of veto.

It seems clear now that Churchill, though one of the chief objects of the Opposition's anger, was not entirely behind Lloyd George in these affairs. The two men never disagreed in public, but there was a limit to how far Churchill would go in deliberately soaking the rich. No doubt at times his dislike of the Tories (and their mutual dislike of him), drove him further to the left than he would naturally have gone. He had an instinctive respect, even an admiration, for the forms and traditions of the prosperous century that had just ended, and he hated to see them attacked in any way.

When he moved from the Board of Trade to the Home Office in 1910 there was some evidence of this slowing down on his liberal course. Strikes occurred in the Welsh coal-mines and on the docks and railways, and Churchill sent special police into the affected areas. It was true that the local authorities had called on the Home Office for help, and bloodshed was avoided, but the action was thought by many people to be a little too precipitate. It affronted the strikers where possibly no need for affront had arisen. It was the beginning, in fact, of a deep-seated distrust of Churchill in his handling of domestic issues which has continued in the trade union movement ever since. If his recent social legislation at the Board of Trade was remembered at all it was regarded now as an act of patronage, a series of half measures doled out as a charity and not given as a right. It was Lloyd George who now stepped in and successfully came to an arrangement with the strikers.

Just one other lesser affair characterised Churchill's short tenure at the Home Office, and it was, in a curiously striking way, symptomatic of his basic approach to politics, perhaps even to life itself—the technique of knocking your opponent hard and then once he is defeated treating him with magnanimity. Two gunmen barricaded themselves in a house in Sidney Street, in the East End of London, and with a supply of bombs and small arms proceeded to fight it out with the police. There were a number of casualties, and in the midst of the fray the Home Secretary appeared in person, top-hatted and astrakhan-collared, to take a hand in the operations, as though he were back again at Omdurman—an action that did not appear like sober statesmanship to the House of Commons. Just what did the Home Secretary think he was doing there with his field guns and the bullets whistling all around? The two gunmen died when their fortress burned down around them, but in the prisons other law-breakers began to find life more bearable. Remembering perhaps his own claustrophobic experiences as a prisoner of war ('I certainly hated every minute of my captivity more than I have ever hated any other period of my whole life'), Churchill introduced a number of reforms into British prisons, and when as Home Secretary he was given the power of reprieving criminals condemned to death he tended to come down on the side of mercy.

First Lord of the Admiralty

In 1911, when he was just thirty-seven years of age, Churchill moved on from the Home Office to the Admiralty and the last chapter of his political youth. In the face of a continuously mounting threat from Germany his job was to prepare the Navy for war, in the same way as Haldane was preparing the Army. Looking back now from the nineteen-sixties it seems that a strangely somnolent air hangs over these last fated years of peace in Europe, at any rate as far as the general public was concerned. The House of Commons was giving most of its attention to Home Rule in Ireland when the Archduke Franz Ferdinand was assassinated at Sarajevo on 28th June 1914 and in any case there was a strong peace party within the Liberal Cabinet itself. Then suddenly everything was rushing down a cascade, and there was no time for Home Rule or peace parties or anything else that belonged to the safe and settled past.

The manner in which Churchill rose to this emergency is certainly one of the most creditable and inspiring things of his whole career. He had made friends long before with Lord Fisher, the retired First Sea Lord, one of the most in-tractable of men, and he had carried through Fisher's programme with the utmost determination. Fisher wanted the fleet to burn oil instead of coal: Churchill pushed through a deal by which for two million pounds the Government obtained a controlling interest in the Anglo-Iranian Oil Company and first call on all its oil in time of war. Fisher wanted more speed and faster ships. Churchill, no longer an apostle of retrenchment, forced the Cabinet to grant the money. Fisher wanted Jellicoe in command of the Grand Fleet, and Churchill put him there, retaining on his own staff as his secretary David Beatty, by now the youngest Admiral in the Navy. In the midst of this, the First Lord found time to promote a few pet interests of his own. Having taken to flying himself in 1913, he set up the Royal Naval Flying Corps, and a year later gave instructions to the naval engineers to look into the possibility of constructing an armoured car which would go over trenches. When later they produced in the Horse Guards Parade one morning a weird contrivance on caterpillar wheels, he approved the design at once, and without waiting for the authority of the Army Council placed orders for eighteen of these new land-ships at the cost of seventy thousand pounds out of Navy funds. This was the beginning of the tank, which was known at that time as 'Winston's folly'.

Then too, the very events of the time appeared to conspire in Churchill's favour. Early in 1914, long before the war was regarded as a definite possibility, he cancelled the usual naval manoeuvres and instead ordered a test mobilisation

1914: The Churchill children, Diana and Randolph, with their nurse in Whitehall.

of the fleet. On 17th and 18th July there was
a review at Spithead, and on Sunday 2nd
August, the day that Germany declared war on
Russia, Churchill on his own initiative had the
ships steaming to their battle stations in the
North Sea. In this act alone there was a
victory for the Entente: the entire British
Expeditionary Force was transported to France
without the loss of a single man.

Churchill moved in these days with an
enormous gusto. He was perfectly at home
with the Navy, and when in this same
November he brought back Fisher as First
Sea Lord the fleet came under the most spirited
control it had known since the days of Nelson.

Of Churchill's own activities it was barely
possible for Asquith or anyone else to keep
track. Within the first few weeks of the opening
of hostilities he was off to Dunkirk to take part

Lady Randolph Churchill (then Mrs Cornwallis-West),
in 1911.

With Mrs Churchill at Hendon aerodrome, in 1914.

'What is your policy?' Notes exchanged between Lloyd George and Churchill across the Cabinet table, 3 August 1914. Churchill answers: 'At the present moment I would act in such a way as to impress Germany with our intention to preserve the neutrality of Belgium.' Lloyd George: 'Would you commit yourself in public now (Monday) to war if Belgium is invaded whether, Belgium asks for our protection or not?' Churchill: 'NO.'

personally in an action on the left flank of the advancing German Army. Then in October, when all Belgium was collapsing and it was vital to hold Antwerp, if only for a few days, he was asked to go over and try to save the situation. He presented himself in the city in the uniform of an elder brother of Trinity House, and at once took charge of the resistance.

Back at the Admiralty he immediately embarked upon an adventure which was bolder than anything that had yet been dreamed of: the forcing of the Dardanelles.

The Gallipoli campaign of 1915 was the most imaginative, the most con‚ *Gallipoli* troversial and—in its possibilities—the most important single operation in the whole course of the two world wars. By the end of 1914 the German onrush across France had been stopped in the Battle of the Marne, and in the east the Russians, though dreadfully hit, were still just able to hold their ground. The Gallipoli campaign was an attempt to break this deadlock, and bring the war to a rapid end by a decisive outflanking movement from the south which would enable the British and the French to join hands with their Russian allies in the Balkans. When it failed Europe was condemned to four senseless years of slaughter in the trenches, from which it has not yet recovered, and in the east there followed the long campaigns in the Mesopotamian desert, the collapse of Russia, the revolution, and the setting up of the Soviet Republic as we know it today.

Within the short nine months of its duration the Gallipoli adventure drew together all the threads of war: the most modern weapons and the greatest ships, the latest inventions like the submarine and the aeroplane, the worst and some of the most brilliant strokes of generalship; and so long as the issue hung in doubt so too did the fate of half a dozen kingdoms and governments.

There was something too in the very setting of the battle—Mount Ida and the ruins of Troy, the Hellespont of Byron and Hero and Leander—that seemed to bring the young soldiers to an extreme pitch of romantic heroism, so that there was nothing which they would not dare and no hopeless prospect of death for which they would not volunteer.

Field-Marshal Lord Kitchener (1850–1916), War Minister 1914–1916.

The campaign was the turning point of Churchill's career. It was not entirely his plan, but he was the chief sponsor of it in the beginning, he kept arguing inside the Cabinet until he got his way, and in the end his reputation was staked upon the outcome.

To Churchill, who was then in 1914 the First Lord of the Admiralty, the issues were clear. The trench warfare in France was getting nowhere, and the German Navy was refusing to come out and fight. Meanwhile you had this wonderful instrument in the British Navy, the most powerful striking weapon in the world, lying virtually idle. If it could blast its way through the Dardanelles to Constantinople it would throw Turkey out of the war, bring the Balkans in on the side of the Allies, and relieve the awful pressure which the German armies just then were bringing to bear on Russia.

But first there were two formidable men to persuade: Lord Kitchener, the Secretary of State for War, and Lord Fisher, the First Sea Lord.

Kitchener in 1914 was something of a demigod in British affairs. No general in the Second World War ever approached his power and influence. The country was covered with the famous recruiting poster that showed his heroic soldierly head, the two fiercely glaring eyes, the pointing finger, and underneath the legend 'Your Country Needs YOU'. In Whitehall he was the oracle of war. Erect, ponderous, self-centred and completely authoritative, he announced his decisions to Cabinet and the War Office.

Fisher, too, occupied a position of great influence. He was already over seventy and was known to be an erratic and somewhat peppery figure, but then it was he more than any other man who had created the Grand Fleet, he radiated energy and ideas, and to the public he was the personification of the British tradition of the sea. It was Churchill who had brought him back from retirement as First Sea Lord soon after the outbreak of the war, and the two men worked together in a close and oddly emotional relationship at the Admiralty.

Little by little Churchill brought Fisher round to the idea of the Dardanelles, until in the end he was positively enthusiastic. Kitchener was less difficult to handle—indeed, he was in favour of some sort of naval action. At this stage, however, he was inclined to think that Gallipoli could never be more than a sideshow. But if the Navy

Admiral Lord Fisher: 'Ruthless, relentless, remorseless.'

wished to 'go it alone', well then, good luck to them; he might be able to spare them a few soldiers to make a landing later on.

In the months that followed Churchill came to be regarded as the interfering amateur who seduced the admirals and the generals into the campaign against their better judgment; he was the reckless adventurer, equally indifferent to the loss of ships and of human life, who persisted in his mad plans long after all hope had gone. Still, after forty years, an echo of that impression remains, faint but insistent, and it is an interesting thing to look briefly into what actually happened.

On 15th January 1915 the Cabinet formally consented to the dispatch of a naval expedition 'to bombard and take the Gallipoli Peninsula with Constantinople as its objective,' and at 9.51 a.m. on 19th February a combined British and French fleet went into action with 178 guns. At first all went well. By the end of the first week the fleet was able to steam six miles up the straits, and was within sight of the critical point, the Narrows at Chanak, where the channel was little more than a mile across; once through this neck another thirty miles would bring them out into the Sea of Marmora. Admiral Carden,

in command of the British and French fleets, sent a signal to London saying that he hoped to get to Constantinople in about fourteen days.

But now delays occurred. Carden fell ill. The opposition stiffened as the expedition advanced, there was much mine-sweeping to be done, and it was not until the morning of 18th March that another full-scale attack was developed. In the meantime, unknown to the Allies, twenty new mines had been laid in Eren Keni Bay on the Asiatic shore—and these twenty mines have a place in history. At 1.54 p.m. an immense explosion was seen on board the French battleship *Bouvet,* and she sank within two minutes. Soon afterwards the *Inflexible* was struck, and there followed in rapid succession the loss of the *Irresistible,* the *Ocean* and the *Gaulois.* No one could make out what was happening.

In this uncertainty Admiral de Robeck, who had succeeded Carden, ordered a withdrawal at 5 p.m., intending however to attack again on the following day. Despite the losses, Churchill in London was all in favour of this course— and indeed, apart from the sinking of the ships the casualties were not very

3 September 1915: the British landing under shell-fire on the beaches of Suvla Bay, Gallipoli.

great: 600 French and barely 60 British. But as the excitement of the action wore off through the night an increasing feeling of doubt and anxiety began to take its place. To veterans like Fisher it was an appalling thing that so many battleships should have been lost so quickly and so mysteriously, and when on the following day de Robeck failed to get promptly under way again he was forbidden to move. For the next month not a single shot was fired on the Gallipoli Peninsula.

Not until nearly four years later, when the war was over, was it learned that the Turkish garrison had been at its last extremity, its stocks of mines and ammunition all but exhausted, and its gunners demoralized by this, the heaviest naval bombardment in history. In Constantinople the Sultan and the government were preparing to decamp with the treasury into Asia Minor, and it was feared that a revolution would break out in the city. 'If the British had only had the courage to rush more ships through the Dardanelles,' Enver Pasha declared, 'they could have got to Constantinople.'

Churchill's quarrel with Fisher dates from this moment. Immediately after the 18th March engagement Fisher announced that he was opposed to any further operations. The whole campaign, he said, had better be abandoned. 'High words,' Churchill says, were used between himself and Fisher, and although the quarrel was patched up for the moment it was clear that it only needed another crisis to cause an open breach.

With Kitchener, however, things were working in precisely the opposite direction. Now suddenly in March he becomes filled with tremendous determination. The Army must now tackle the job. The Australian and New Zealand troops which have recently arrived in Egypt are to be diverted to the scene, together with the British 29th Division; and he sends for General Ian Hamilton.

Hamilton was a devoted and scholarly figure, one of the long succession of British poet-generals, an experienced man but perhaps not a dynamic one. He was told to go off post-haste and organise a full-scale landing on the enemy fortress. He was given no plan—and there were no plans because this was almost the first that anyone in the War Office had heard about a Gallipoli landing. Kitchener did not discuss his plans: he announced them. Hamilton had no staff, no intelligence of the enemy strength or dispositions, no maps and no clear directive, but off he went by express train across France and thence by fast cruiser to the scene of operations.

After 18th March the Turks began to fortify the peninsula with all possible speed. They got guns from the Skoda works. They sent down sixty thousand men to dig themselves in behind barbed wire and sighted machine-guns. They appointed Liman von Sanders, a German general of exceptional drive and tenacity, to take command.

All this was thoroughly known or guessed at in Egypt, where Hamilton was assembling his force; but still the decision was taken to go ahead. Moreover, there was no secret about the new army's destination. It was openly talked about in Cairo. It was mentioned in the newspapers. And the expedition itself was labelled 'The Constantinople Force'; letters from home bearing that address were delivered to the troops. All mystery, except actual tactical surprise, having thus been taken out of the proceedings, both sides set about their preparations as on some battlefield in the Middle Ages.

Churchill's course through these bemused events was clearer than most. He was never a great enthusiast for the land operation. He always believed that the Navy could have done the job alone, at any rate in the early stages. But now with this new enthusiasm of Kitchener's, events were very largely taken out of his hands. In public and to a great extent in the semi-privacy of Whitehall he was still regarded as the Minister who was primarily responsible for the undertaking, and he was still eager for it, provided only that the Army acted quickly and with a sufficient number of men. Through the rest of March and April he was constantly at Kitchener's door urging more and more haste, offering additional ships if only Kitchener would supply the additional men.

But here he was up against massive opposition. To Joffre, the French Commander-in-Chief, and the British Army Staff the only way to win the war was to 'wear down the Boches' in France; Gallipoli, to them, was a wasteful and dangerous diversion of men and supplies. In consequence the eastern front was always a poor relation, and it became the classic example of the tragedy of too little and too late. In the end half a million men were committed piecemeal to the battle, and they were forever doomed to see the victory slipping away just an inch beyond their grasp.

This being said, the rest of the story is marvellous. A splendour falls on Gallipoli; in this present age of nuclear fission nothing quite so grand is likely to pass our way again. The fleet that steamed out of Mudros on the night of 24th April 1915, against the background of Mount Athos and the Grecian islands, must have been one of the most majestic sights of all maritime warfare. Both sailors and soldiers were possessed with that kind of reckless confidence that can only come through inexperience and the emotion of sharing a tremendous risk together. By dawn the Army was ashore at three places. They ran headlong into machine-gun fire, and their losses were considerably more than at the D-day landing in Normandy thirty years later. Never on this first day, nor in any of the Homeric battles ahead, did they succeed in advancing more than a few thousand yards inland.

When the first rage of these opening battles was over, and the losses on either side were already being numbered in tens of thousands, General Hamilton could claim that he was still ashore, but nothing more. Even so he had come very near success. Had Liman von Sanders not taken a chance and boldly committed the bulk of his forces at once, and had not a fanatical young general named Mustapha Kemal taken charge in the firing line, the British almost certainly would have broken through and gained the heights. But by the middle of May it was apparent that all impetus was lost. Hamilton wrote home to Kitchener that unless he was reinforced he could do no more.

The effect of this news in England was to precipitate a major crisis. On 12th May Fisher pressed for the immediate return of the *Queen Elizabeth* from the Dardanelles, and had a violent row with Kitchener in consequence. On 14th May there was a despondent Cabinet meeting. Fisher now announced that he had been opposed to the Dardanelles operation from the beginning, and that in no circumstances would he agree to the renewal of the naval attack until the Army had won the peninsula. Despite this outburst, it seemed to Churchill

Churchill's tribute to Rupert Brooke who died in the Dardanelles campaign.

Andrew Bonar Law (1858–1923).
He enforced Churchill's dismissal
from the Admiralty.

that he and Fisher parted on fairly good terms that night.
But on the following day Fisher resigned.

The Admiral's resignation was not something which
the Liberal Government could pass over as simply
another change of command. Coming on top of so many
other troubles the Conservatives were up in arms about
it, and Asquith's position became impossible. On 18th
May he began conversations with Bonar Law, the
leader of the Conservative Opposition, with the object
of setting up a coalition government.

The Conservatives were perfectly willing to come
in, but upon one point they were adamant. Under no
conditions whatever would they have Churchill back at
the Admiralty or in any other senior ministry. This
was more than a little ruthless, to say the least of it, since
Churchill had had no responsibility for the military
operations at Gallipoli; they were undertaken on Kitchener's initiative and with the support of the War Cabinet. A
personal appeal to Bonar Law by Churchill himself still
made no difference; the best offer Asquith could make to
him was the Colonies, which Churchill refused. He
agreed eventually to take the Duchy of Lancaster, with
a seat on the Dardanelles Committee. The Admiralty
went to Balfour. It was by some way the worst set-back
of Churchill's career.

Ashmead-Bartlett, the war correspondent, who had
returned from the Dardanelles, gives a revealing glimpse
of Churchill at this moment. They had dined together
at Churchill's mother's house, and after a stormy argument
were walking home at midnight through the dark and
almost deserted streets.

'We reached Admiralty House, where he is staying
at the request of Mr Balfour until his own town house
is ready, and he let me in through a narrow side door.
The rooms, where he had passed so many days of power,
were now deserted. A single attendant was on duty, and
he got soundly abused for not answering the bell immediately. Winston wandered through the rooms, in which he
is now only living on sufferance, his head bent, his face
flushed, his hands behind his back, picking up a book
here, a letter there, glancing at them and throwing them
aside, his mind unable to concentrate upon anything but

the Dardanelles. The ornate rooms and official papers seemed to mock him; the deserted hall so lately full of sycophants, admirers and place-seekers now only re-echoed to the sound of his own voice. He presented the perfect picture of a fallen Minister. Once again he cried out in the silent night, "They [the Admiralty, the Cabinet], never fought it out to a finish. They never gave my schemes a fair trial".'

There is a nightmarish quality about the rest of the Gallipoli story, and it need not be examined here in any detail, as Churchill ceased to exert a major influence upon it. He was in the maddening position of being held to blame for every reverse without having the power to affect the decisions that were taken.

Finally on 31st October General Munro, who had replaced Hamilton as Commander-in-Chief, dispatched a telegram recommending the total evacuation of the Gallipoli Peninsula and the final abandonment of the campaign. He reckoned on the loss of some forty thousand men.

Kitchener, thunderstruck by this advice, hurried out to Gallipoli himself, and after a final series of waverings agreed that it must be so.

In the event the actual evacuation turned out to be a fantastic success. Despite the winter storms which washed the jetties away, and the constant watchfulness of the Turks, the soldiers were brought off with hardly a casualty. The Turks came forward cautiously in the morning to find the beaches empty and vast piles of stores and ammunition burning on the shore. It was all over.

Could it ever have succeeded? In the forty-odd years that have since elapsed Churchill's view seems in the main to have been vindicated. Certainly if anyone in 1915 could have foreseen the battles of extermination in France in the ensuing three years, and the Russian revolution of 1917, there would have been more readiness to find the guns and the men for Gallipoli. Certainly if there had been a combined operation in the first place—if Kitchener had sent a couple of divisions to make a landing when the fleet was first bombarding the straits in February 1915—the Dardanelles must surely have been opened. Whether or not the fleet alone could have got through is a more difficult proposition; and here the weight of opinion seems to have gone against Churchill.

In the end one imagines it was very largely a question of

Churchill's letter of resignation from the Asquith Government, as published in *The Times*, 13 November, 1915.

MR. CHURCHILL RESIGNS.

NO PLACE IN WAR COUNCIL.

CABINET WORK AT AN END.

OFFER TO SERVE IN THE FIELD.

Mr. Churchill has resigned his office of Chancellor of the Duchy of Lancaster, and has placed himself at the disposal of the military authorities, his regiment being now in France.

The following is the text of the letters which have passed between him and Mr. Asquith :—

November 11, 1915.

My dear Asquith,—When I left the Admiralty five months ago, I accepted an office with few duties in order, at your request, to take part in the work of the War Council and to assist new Ministers with the knowledge of current operations which I then possessed in a special degree. The counsels which I have offered are upon record in the minutes of the Committee of Imperial Defence and in the Memoranda I have circulated to the Cabinet, and I draw your attention at the present time to these.

I am in cordial agreement with the decision to form a small War Council. I appreciated the intention you expressed to me six weeks ago to include me among its members. I foresaw then the personal difficulties which you would have to face in its composition, and I make no complaint at all that your scheme should be changed. But with that change my work in the Government comes naturally to a close.

Knowing what I do about the present situation and the instrument of Executive power, I could not accept a position of general responsibility for war policy without any effective share in its guidance and control. Even when decisions of principle are rightly taken the speed and method of their execution are factors which determine the result. Nor do I feel able, in times like these, to remain in well-paid inactivity. I therefore ask you to submit my resignation to the King. I am an officer, and I place myself unreservedly at the disposal of the Military authorities, observing that my regiment is in France.

I have a clear conscience, which enables me to bear my responsibility for past events with composure.

Time will vindicate my administration of the Admiralty, and assign me my due share in the vast series of preparations and operations which have secured us the command of the seas.

With much respect and unaltered personal friendship, I bid you good-bye.

Yours very sincerely,
WINSTON S. CHURCHILL.
November 12, 1915.

In France, 1915: with General Fayolle at the Headquarters of the French 33rd Corps.

faith, and at the time there were not enough people like Churchill who really believed in the expedition. It was not so much a matter of judgment as of resolution. Churchill's own summing-up of the affair is that he made the mistake of committing himself to the enterprise when he did not have the personal authority to push it through. One feels there is something in this. Had he then been Prime Minister, or even had Fisher and Kitchener gone from the scene a few months earlier, we might have had Constantinople.

As it happened, however, Churchill's reputation sank steadily with the news of every fresh set-back on the peninsula. He was already disliked by the Tories for his politics, and now he was generally despised for his judgment. To Lord Riddell, who saw him at this time, he said, 'I am finished'. 'Not at forty,' said Riddell. But yes, Churchill insisted, he was the victim of a political intrigue and everything he cared for was gone.

Resignation   By November 1915 he could not stand it any longer. The House listened coldly to the speech in which he resigned from his minor office of Chancellor of the Duchy of Lancaster, and accepted without much feeling the news that he was off to France to fight in the trenches.

A few days later, in a cold November rain, Major Churchill presented himself to his colonel in the Grenadier Guards, the regiment with which he was to have a month's experience before receiving a command of his own. The battalion was just on the point of taking over in the line. As a discredited politician of anti-Tory views, the man held responsible for Gallipoli, Churchill did not cut much of a figure at that time and place, and for half an hour he was ignored. The Colonel then felt himself permitted to make an observation.

'I think I ought to tell you,' he said, 'that we were not consulted at all on the matter of your coming to join us.'

Churchill spent six months in the trenches in France in 1916, and it was not until a year later —a year in which he was at a very low ebb, defending his name before the Commission of Inquiry into the Dardanelles—that Lloyd George felt his reputation was sufficiently restored for him to be reinstated in office. But the post that was found for him—the Ministry of Munitions—was one of the best. It was a vast organisation, charged not only with supplying the British forces with weapons and ammunition, but the recently arrived American Army as well. It must have been a particular satisfaction for Churchill to produce the new tanks, the Big Willies, which had been so derided when he first pressed for their development in the early days of the war.

On 20th November 1917, at Cambrai, 378 of these tanks with 98 auxiliaries were sent into attack without a preliminary artillery bombardment which would have destroyed the element of surprise. The Germans broke on a six-mile front, and ten thousand prisoners were taken. It was the first decisive victory in France, the beginning of the ending of the war. When it was all over the Royal Commission investigating the claims of inventors appended this note to their report:

'In the first phase the Commission desire to record their view that it was primarily due to the receptivity, courage and driving force of the Rt Hon. Winston Spencer-Churchill that the general idea of the use of such an instrument of

The front line at Ovillers, Somme, 1916.

A British tank on the French front, 1916.

'Too little and too late': the evacuation of Gallipoli, January 1916.

warfare as the tank was converted into practical shape, but Mr Churchill has very properly taken the view that all his thought and time belonged to the State and that he was not entitled to make any claim for an award, even if he had liked to do so. But it seems proper that the above view should be recorded by way of tribute to Mr Winston Churchill.'

His other special interest was in the air. In the later days of the war he developed a habit of rising early, completing his work at the Ministry in the morning and then flying over to France to see how things were going at the front during the afternoon. He was back in time to resume work again in England in the evening. At the present time this would be eccentric; in 1918 it was very nearly suicidal. Once his machine caught fire over the Channel; on another occasion it somersaulted at the take-off. Then again a little later, when he was piloting himself, the guiding stick failed and he crashed a hundred feet on to Croydon aerodrome. He stepped out of the debris and was addressing the House of Commons two hours later. He was already then approaching fifty.

Minister under Lloyd George

In the four years following the election at the end of the war Churchill served under Lloyd George in two Cabinet posts, first as Secretary of State for War and for the Air, and then as Minister for the Colonies. His record is distinguished by three acts of pacification and two acts of the utmost provocation.

His pacifying acts would hardly now be criticised by any party. There was an absurd scheme in the Army for first demobilising 'key' men—mechanics and such—who would put British industry back on its feet. Even those who had been only a few months in the ranks were given preference, and among the

Returning home from a quick trip to France.

Crossing Portsmouth Harbour in an Army biplane, 1914.

millions of older men still left in the garrisons of England, Scotland and France, open mutiny broke out. The situation was getting out of control when Churchill came to the War Office. He quashed the key-men plan, gave preference to the wounded and the long-service soldiers, and increased the pay of those who were bound to wait some time for their release.

He was equally successful in 1920 in getting a settlement in the Middle East, where a chaotic situation had developed from the break-up of the Turkish Empire. Rebellion had broken out in Iraq. Calling a conference in Cairo with T. E. Lawrence as his chief adviser, Churchill established Feisal on the throne in Iraq and his brother as the Emir Abdullah in Transjordan. The British Army in Iraq (which was costing forty million pounds a year), was replaced by an RAF garrison—a saving of some thirty-five millions. The settlement has largely continued to the present day.

Churchill's other success was in Ireland. The Irish question which so bedevilled British politics for a century or more is already beginning to recede, like some half-forgotten nightmare, into the perspective of history. But in the early nineteen-twenties it seemed at times that this issue eclipsed every other and

Michael Collins: 'He acted up to his word.'   Lawrence of Arabia: 'One mind, one soul, one will-power.'

that there could be no solution of it. The Treaty of 1921 which Churchill as Secretary of State for the Colonies helped to negotiate, and which he piloted through the House of Commons, was the first real beginning of the Irish peace. It set up the Irish Free State with its own government under Arthur Griffith and Michael Collins, and although the fearful civil war continued a little longer that treaty has been the basis of the Irish settlement ever since.

The provocative acts touched on two of the main themes of his political life, and it is doubtful if we have seen the end of these issues even yet. In 1918 Lenin and the Bolsheviks held Moscow and the central regions of Russia. They were the declared enemies of the Allies, since they had agreed to a separate peace with Germany and were at open war with the White Russian leaders who wanted to carry on the struggle. These leaders—Admiral Denikin, General Koltchak and General Wrangel—had control in the outer provinces and were supported in Russia by a force of some 25,000 British, American, French and Italian troops. Three thousand White Russian officers were being trained by the British at Vladivostok and quantities of arms were being sent in through Murmansk and Archangel. Until the Germans were defeated the policy of the Allies was perfectly clear: they were bound to do all they could to defeat the Bolsheviks, since for all practical purposes the Bolsheviks had joined the German side.

After the armistice it was a different matter. Should you let the Russians settle their own affairs (which was, broadly, the policy of Lloyd George and Woodrow Wilson), or should you continue your support of the White Russians, who had been your allies in the war and were now being exterminated (which was Churchill's policy)?

Churchill was not at all disinterested in this matter. In the past, and at every point in his career, he had been blindingly clear about his personal loathing of the Marxist regime. His diatribe on Lenin (and it was Lenin who counted then, not Stalin), is one of the most devastating—or, if you like, diabolic—pieces of vituperation in his whole repertoire; and he was never exactly an amateur in this field.

'In the middle of April 1917 the Germans took a sombre decision. Ludendorff refers to it with bated breath. Full allowance must be made for the desperate stakes to which the German leaders were already committed. They were in the mood which had opened unlimited submarine warfare with the certainty of bringing the United States into the war against them. Upon the Western front they had from the beginning used the most terrible means of offence at their disposal. They had employed poison gas on the largest scale and had invented the 'Flammenwerfer'. Nevertheless it was with a sense of awe that they turned

1919: With his daughter at the march past of the Guards at Buckingham Palace.

War Minister Churchill
with Field-Marshal
Sir Henry Wilson,
inspecting British
troops in the
Rhineland.

upon Russia the most grisly of all weapons. They transported Lenin in a sealed
truck like a plague bacillus from Switzerland into Russia.'

It was, then, with a certain amount of personal approbation, that Churchill
as Minister for War set about dispatching another 8,000 men and further
supplies to Russia. If the worst came to the worst it was thought that this contingent would, at any rate, be useful in covering the withdrawal of the Allied
troops.

But England was exhausted in 1919, and there was a strong feeling that the
Bolsheviks should be left alone. Although Churchill was by no means the
principal minister for steering Cabinet policy on Russia, the outcry that followed was directed, as so often before, upon his name. In the end the troops were
withdrawn, and Russia from that moment was sealed off from the West in
much the same way as China became sealed off thirty years later.

The other incident appeared at the time to be even more serious. Under the
Treaty of Sèvres, Turkey had accepted the break-up of her empire, and a
garrison of British, French and Italians was stationed in Constantinople and
along a strip of the Dardanelles at Chanak. In 1920 Mustapha Kemal at the
head of a patriotic force of irregulars repudiated this treaty, and a Greek army,
to some extent encouraged by Lloyd George and the Allies, advanced into

Anatolia against him. At the end of a fourteen-day battle at Sakkaria the Greeks were routed, and after a short truce Kemal continued his advance to the west, apparently intending to cross into Europe. Churchill had not been an avid supporter of Lloyd George's Greek policy, but he was determined that the Allied garrison should not be defied and overrun with the result perhaps that all the Balkans would be thrown into war again. He proposed, therefore, that reinforcements should be sent to Sir Charles Harington, the British Commander in Constantinople, and that the British fleet, on proceeding to the Sea of Marmora, should be instructed to open fire if necessary. At the same time France, Italy and the British Dominions were also invited to send new contingents to Turkey 'to safeguard all that has been gained in war'.

A communiqué along these lines was prepared by Churchill at the request of the Prime Minister and his colleagues. It went far beyond the point that almost anyone was prepared to go, and immediately a storm broke out. Was war to start again and at that same fatal point, the Dardanelles? Poincaré, the French Premier, meanwhile had withdrawn the French contingent. In England the Conservatives under Bonar Law protested that England could not act as 'policeman of the world', and the peace party turned strongly against Churchill. Already there was a feeling in the country that the Coalition Government under Lloyd George had continued too long, and this new incident was the *coup de grâce*. It did not matter that the Government's policy in fact turned out to be, for

Playing polo at Roehampton, 1923.

a time at any rate, a brilliant success: Kemal withdrew his forces from Chanak and a settlement was arranged. At their famous meeting in the Carlton Club on 19th October 1922, the Conservatives by 187 votes to 87 decided to with-draw their support from the Coalition. A mild attempt by Churchill and Austen Chamberlain to create a Centre Party against the Socialists came to nothing, and a change in government was then inevitable. Thus the Coalition of Liberals and Tories which had been created by a crisis in the Dardanelles in 1915 was now demolished, seven years later, by the same cause.

Bonar Law took office with a Conservative Cabinet in 1922. At the ensuing election the Conservatives came in with a clear majority. Lloyd George was out, never to return to high office again. Churchill even lost his seat at Dundee; when the votes were counted it was found that he was at the bottom of the poll with the Communist candidate, Mr William Gallagher. He was recuperating from an appendicitis operation at the time, and he remarked a little ruefully that he found himself 'without an office, without a seat, without a party and without an appendix'. He went off with his wife to winter in the south of France, where he had rented a villa, Le Rève d'Or, near Cannes. It was the first time he had been out of the House for more than twenty years.

But it was the weakening of his ties with the Liberal Party, or rather the weakening of the Liberal Party itself, which was the really serious issue for Churchill. He was committed now to the belief that a strong Opposition force must be formed against the Labour Party and the Communists (whom he lumped together), and that function was rapidly being taken over from the Liberals by his old party the Conservatives.

The break finally came in 1924. In the new election that year the composition of the House was as follows: Baldwin and the Conservatives, 255 seats, Asquith and the Liberals, 158, Ramsay Macdonald and Labour, 191. When Asquith decided to give his support to Macdonald and thus set up the first Labour Government in British history, Churchill parted from the Liberals for ever. Labour were his opponents; there was no choice now but to return to the Conservatives.

Meanwhile, far from influencing these changes of government, he was finding it extremely difficult to get back into the House at all. In 1923 he stood for Leicester West and was easily defeated by Pethick Lawrence, the Socialist candidate. In the following year he stood as an Independent (with strong Con-servative leanings) for the Abbey Division of Westminster, and although it was first announced that he had 'won by a hundred', the final count revealed that in a poll of 22,000 he had lost by 43 votes. He had now had three defeats in a row, and he had been out of the House for nearly two years.

In retrospect Churchill's changes of party do not appear as illogical or irres-ponsible actions. He was always a Free Trader, and it was only when the Con-servatives abandoned Free Trade that he turned away from them in 1904 to join the Liberal Party. He was always an opponent of Socialism, and it was only

1924: At work with his secretary during the Abbey by-election fight.

Mr and Mrs Churchill outside the Committee Rooms in the Abbey by-election.

Stanley Baldwin (1876–1947), Prime Minister: 'He had a genius for waiting upon events.'

when the Liberals joined the Socialists in 1924 that he returned to the Conservatives. Equally his exploits and policies early in the war, especially at Antwerp and Gallipoli, were, in the light of all that has since happened, the expression of a rational and most resourceful mind.

But these things did not seem like that at the time. The changes of party represented to many voters merely instability and opportunism; and his military adventures were seen only as failures causing terrible losses of men. And so at these elections he was met with cries of, 'What about Antwerp? What about the Dardanelles?' and accusations of having 'ratted'. Only his courage and known brilliance were unquestioned, though even these might not have been enough had he not also been tenacious. He stood for election again in 1924 when the Macdonald administration fell, and this time the Epping division of Essex brought him in on the Conservative landslide with a solid majority.

Return to the Conservative Party

Baldwin, now firmly in power with a majority of 211, saw with some shrewdness that if he was going to have Churchill at all he had better have him where he belonged—at the top. He offered him the Chancellorship of the Exchequer. Churchill had not expected anything half so grand as this—indeed, there is a story that at first he thought he was being offered not the Chancellorship of the Exchequer but the Chancellorship of the Duchy of Lancaster—and he at once accepted. For the next five years he brought in the Conservative Budget.

James Ramsay MacDonald,
Britain's first Labour Prime Minister
whom Churchill called
'the boneless wonder'.

Churchill's chancellorship was in many ways his least successful period in office, and it is chiefly remembered for two issues which might have brought the country near to disaster: the return to the gold standard and the general strike that followed.

Britain had gone off the gold standard as a result of the war, and the pound in consequence had fallen to about ninety per cent of its value in 1914. In the mid-twenties, when Churchill first came to the Treasury, there was strong pressure both from the City and from his own advisers to restore the pound to its old credit by going back on to gold again. The manifest danger of this policy was that the pound would become such a hard currency that British manufacturers would have difficulty in selling their goods abroad—unless of course they cut prices, and the only way of doing that was by reducing wages. Nevertheless it was decided that the credit of the pound was all-important and the risk had to be taken.

It was J. M. Keynes who set out the dangers of this course with brutal and ironic clarity in his pamphlet *The Economic Consequences of Mr Churchill*, which was published after the decision was taken. Having in one lapidary phrase demolished the advice of the Treasury experts as 'vague and jejeune meditations', he went on to warn Churchill that he was committing himself to a policy of cutting wages and reducing the standard of living by deliberately creating unemployment; and this was certain to lead to industrial disputes.

John Maynard Keynes
(1883–1946).

In fairness it ought to be remembered that it was not Churchill who initiated the policy of returning to gold: it was his predecessor, the Labour Chancellor, Snowden. However, the consequences very quickly followed. For a while the Government managed to keep up miners' wages by the payment of subsidies to the coal-owners, but these subsidies could not be maintained. In the face of this the owners had no choice but to reduce wages, and with that the miners came out on strike, bringing the workers of many other industries with them.

The general strike which began on 4th May 1926 and continued for nearly a fortnight (though the miners were not starved back to work for another six months) remains one of the most serious episodes in British social history. Apart from its economic consequences (it is said to have cost the country £800 million), and the immense effect it has had on all elections and labour-employer relationships since then, one of its most interesting aspects was that it brought out into the open the personal struggle between Churchill and Ernest Bevin, the leader of the strikers. In the years that followed, these two men perhaps more than any others were responsible for bringing the country together in war and then dividing it again in peace. In their utterly different backgrounds and in their conflicting outlook they were almost absurdly characteristic of their opposing parties and of England; and, being enemies, they were friends. It was no

The General Strike, 1926:
volunteer bus drivers in London
with police protection.

Strikers watching a bus
being towed away.

The British Gazette

Published by His Majesty's Stationery Office.

No. 1. LONDON, WEDNESDAY, MAY 5, 1926. ONE PENNY

FIRST DAY OF GREAT STRIKE

Not So Complete as Hoped by its Promoters

PREMIER'S AUDIENCE OF THE KING

Miners and the General Council Meet at House of Commons

The great strike began yesterday. There are already signs, however, that it is by no means so complete as its promoters hoped. There were far more trains running than was the case on the first day of the railway strike in 1919.

The King received the Prime Minister in audience at Buckingham Palace yesterday morning.

Reports from all parts of the country indicate that satisfactory arrangements have been set up for recruiting. Volunteers came forward in large numbers in London and all the important provincial centres.

STRIKE LEADERS' MEETINGS.

The strike leaders were busy all day, and the mail bag of wires home.

For Londoners to the miners' Federation was a meeting yesterday morning at some headquarters. There was joint urging of all sections, and the officials met later in the day.

A MUSHROOM TOWN

The services of some of these volunteers were maintained in large rule works, owing to the general position.

SPIRIT OF PUBLIC SERVICE.

RECRUITING STATIONS.

The recruiting recruiting stations all volunteers in the London and are open.

NEVER-ENDING QUEUE.

FOOD SUPPLIES

No Hoarding A Fair Share for Everybody

The Government is endeavouring to see that every person has a fair share of food and it is therefore of the greatest importance that every member of the public should assist in maintaining a fair distribution of supplies. They should do this by refraining from buying more than their usual quantities of food stuffs.

Retailers should co-operate in securing a fair distribution of their stocks.

MILK DISTRIBUTION

Control of Supplies in the Metropolis

LAW COURTS AT WORK

Judge on the Duty of the Public

LONDONERS' TREK TO WORK.

G.P.O. SERVICES

Restrictions on Telegrams and Letters

THE KING RECEIVES THE PREMIER

HOLD-UP OF THE NATION

Government and the Challenge

NO FLINCHING

The Constitution or a Soviet

When King and People understand each other past a doubt,
It takes a foe and more than a foe to knock that country out.

— Be strong and quit yourselves like men.

— Kipling.

The general strike is in operation, expressing in no uncertain terms a direct challenge to organised government.

FEW LIGHT HEARTS

THE CHOICE

"The country and Parliament, which represents the nation, are confronted quite simply with the choice either of being masters of submitting to pay forty-six years of the taxpayers' money in one particular form which way the country..."

COMMUNIST LEADER ARRESTED

Mr. Saklatvala, M.P., Charged at Bow Street

SEQUEL TO MAY DAY SPEECH

Mr. Shapurji Saklatvala, the Communist Member of Parliament for North Battersea, was arrested on Monday afternoon on a warrant charging him with inciting his power to commit a breach of the peace arising out of a speech which he made on May-day in Hyde Park.

GOVERNMENT'S VIEW

"It is the view of the Government that their first duty is to keep law and order," continued Sir Travers.

SPECIAL CONSTABLES

Appeal to Capable Citizens in London to Enrol

RESERVE OF OFFICERS

The Deputy Chief Civil Commissioner's Office issues the following:—

THE "BRITISH GAZETTE" AND ITS OBJECTS

Reply to Strike Makers' Plan to Paralyse Public Opinion

REAL MEANING OF THE STRIKE

Conflict Between Trade Union Leaders and Parliament

A few words are needed to explain the appearance of the "British Gazette."

There are at present two quite different disputes which are holding up the country. The first is the stoppage in the coal industry. This is a trade dispute which could be settled in the ordinary way.

NO SECTIONAL DICTATION

NO ADVANCE ON JULY

DANGER OF RUMOURS.

PROSPERITY AT STAKE.

The Chancellor of the
Exchequer lampooned.

THE NEW BRITANNIA

("*Let Britannia*," concluded *Mr. Churchill*, "*cast off the ridiculous and dishonourable disguise and rags made in Germany and in Russia with which the Socialists seek to drape her. Let her reveal herself once again, sedate, majestic on her throne.*") (*Loud Cheers*)

accident that the one man in the silk hat and the other in the cloth cap were never known to the cartoonists, the Press, the House and the public as Bevin and Churchill, but simply as Ernie and Winston; and in England each man's nature was perfectly understood.

Churchill's part in the strike was brisk, forthright and successful. He took over the presses of the *Morning Post* with volunteer labour and produced the *British Gazette* almost as if it were a battle operation. With tremendous drive he marshalled the newsprint, the printers and the necessary transport. With his first issue he got 230,000 copies off the press, and in the remaining eight days of its existence the paper increased its circulation by ten times. As an editor he adopted a fighting attitude which would have been much approved by his grandfather, Leonard Jerome, who exerted great influence on the strong policy of the *New York Times* during the American Civil War—that is to say, Churchill barricaded the doors and let fly with everything he had. And when at the end of the strike he emerged flushed and victorious to relax for an hour at the old Empire Theatre (Adele and Fred Astaire were appearing in *Lady Be Good*), the audience rose and gave him an ovation.

The first issue of the *British Gazette*.

With the Duke of Sutherland at Deauville, 1927.

But this glow did not persist. When the Labour Government of 1929 was succeeded by the Baldwin-Macdonald Coalition in 1931 there was no place for a man who was always at his best in action and determined to possess a cause. England was sinking into the long slow trough of the thirties; the financial depression left people without energy or design, and they were in no mood for causes. Macdonald's plans for disarmament and Baldwin's theme of business as usual were probably a faithful reflection of what the country wanted, and to many people it seemed that Churchill was a toublesome anachronism. For ten years he remained on the back benches, a restless and independent one-man Opposition. To the public he presented a picture of the promising politician who had lost his chance, the brilliant speaker who was never quite sound enough. He was moving steadily now into the position of being a permanent parliamentary celebrity, amusing, contentious and forever out of step.

But there is a pattern in the background. He has two bases and he never deserts them. In the House of Commons he makes his speeches, at home he writes his books, and no matter what happens, whether he is in or out of office, voting with the Conservatives or against them, he is always to be found at one or the other occupation. At no moment is he ever drawn to any other kind of life; the promises of governorships and big business never distract him and never apparently does he entertain any serious notions of retirement. In the midst of so many outward upheavals he is the least displaced person one could possibly imagine.

So now at the beginning of the nineteen-thirties, when it is apparent that there is no place for him in any public office, he turns back naturally to his private life at home; and there he sets the dynamo running as it has never run before. Churchill had never been financially secure like Balfour and so many of his Conservative contemporaries—he had to work and fight for almost everything he achieved. The twenty-odd thousand pounds he had made from his lectures and books early in the century had already been spent, but he was always a highly paid journalist (the *Sunday Pictorial*, for example, offered him £500 apiece for six articles, a very large sum for those days), and Cabinet salaries were much more valuable than they are now. Then in 1919 he unexpec-

Budget Day 1928.

tedly inherited a legacy of some £40,000 from his great-grandmother, the Marchioness of Londonderry. His income rose to about £5,000 a year. Even so he was in financial difficulties at times, and he was not a wealthy man when the Second World War broke out.

In the early nineteen-twenties, after a spell of nearly fifteen years, he returned to his writing. Between 1923 and 1929 four volumes of *The World Crisis* appeared. This was his personal narrative of the First World War and the events leading up to it, and it was a staggering thing that he could have produced so clear and so authoritative a work while, for a time at least, he was still

Chartwell Manor
which Churchill bought
in 1922.

in office. It was then and still is an immense success. Part of the £40,000 he obtained from it was invested in Chartwell Manor, at Westerham in Kent, where he still lives.

His mother, Lady Randolph Churchill, who had survived her husband by a quarter of a century and who twice remarried, died in 1921, but he was surrounded now by his own rising family of four children. Chartwell seems to have been more of a village than a family home, and its activity was never ending. Apart from the children there was a considerable population of cats, dogs, geese, chickens and goldfish; and hardly a day went by that Mrs Churchill was not entertaining. Many of the leading political figures came down from London, and a stream of information and ideas was constantly flowing into the house, so that it became in a way a kind of private cabinet of its own.

His painting went steadily forward, mostly landscapes, flower pieces and the like. Then, taking out a union card as a bricklayer, Churchill constructed two large cottages and a swimming pool. His rate of work was a brick a minute.

But the centre of his private life was now his writing. Churchill wrote as few authors care to do; that is to say, he seldom wrote at all, but instead dictated through the morning to a secretary, producing three or four thousand words a day, an astonishing quantity. In 1930, well within a year of losing office, he brought out *My Early Life*, a simple and delightful account of his first twenty-six years, probably the most pleasant thing he has ever written. There followed one or two volumes of collected essays, and then in the early nineteen-thirties he embarked on a major production, his study of his ancestor Marlborough.

Historians and military experts were brought in to advise and gather the facts. With Professor Lindemann (later to become Lord Cherwell, his adviser on scientific matters), he toured Marlborough's battlefields on the Continent. A painstaking search was made of all contemporary documents at Blenheim and elsewhere. For a period of half a dozen years the intense labour went on, and it has resulted in one of the major historical works of the first half of the present century. One can only note again with awe that so great a project—it

Mending the roof of a cottage at Chartwell.

was published in four volumes—was carried through despite all his other activities, for he was constantly in the House of Commons, entering into every major debate. It may be that he was helped by the very deadness of the times. 'The thirties,' A. L. Rowse has remarked, 'were the heyday of the second rate.' The combination of Baldwin, Macdonald and Neville Chamberlain in the series of governments that ran through from 1931 to 1939 could hardly have seemed to Churchill—and no doubt to Lloyd George as well—as anything less than disastrous.

Churchill put his thoughts to the House perhaps most effectively in his ferocious attack on Ramsay Macdonald:

'I spoke the other day, after he had been defeated in an important division, about his wonderful skill in falling without hurting himself. He falls, but up he comes again, smiling, a little dishevelled but still smiling. But this is a juncture, a situation which will try to the very fullest the particular art in which he excels. I remember when I was a child being taken to the celebrated Barnum's Circus, which contained an exhibition of freaks and monstrosities, but the exhibit of the programme which I most desired to see was the one described as "The Boneless Wonder". My parents judged that the spectacle would be too revolting and demoralising for my youthful eyes, and I have waited fifty years to see the Boneless Wonder sitting on the Treasury Bench.'

John Churchill, first Duke of Marlborough. Churchill's biography of his famous ancestor, written in 1933–1938, won him in 1953 the Nobel Prize for Literature.

But it was over India that Churchill chose from 1931 onwards to open up the gulf once more between himself and the Conservative leaders. Against every party in the House he fought obstinately and often fiercely for the retention of British rule. To go, he kept repeating, meant civil war and the break-up of the Empire. The spectacle of Gandhi affronted him. It was 'alarming and also nauseating to see Mr Gandhi, a seditious Middle Temple lawyer, now posing as a fakir or a type well-known in the East, striding half-naked up the steps of the Viceregal Palace'.

His views had no real support outside a minority in the Conservative Party. The India Bill, which promised Dominion status, went through, and once again Churchill was left crying in the wilderness.

" YAH, UNTOUCHABLE ! "

Churchill denouncing Baldwin's India Policy: 'India is an abstraction! It is no more a united nation than the Equator.'

He was even more at odds with almost everyone over the abdication crisis. Already it is becoming a little difficult to remember the curious sick-room hush that settled over England when it was first learned in December 1936 that King Edward was determined to abdicate, since, as King, he was not able to marry Mrs Simpson. There was great sympathy for the King, but the sense of the proprieties personified by Mr Baldwin and the Archbishop of Canterbury was even greater. When finally the abdication was announced by the Speaker on 10th December, there was a deep feeling of gratitude towards the Prime Minister throughout the country.

Churchill went wildly against the grain in all this. With Baldwin's permission, he saw the King and tendered him advice. He took up the King's cause in the House, asking mildly enough that no decision should be taken until Parliament had discussed the matter. The only effect of this was to foment the idea that he was attempting to create an independent King's Party; and he

May 1933: with his wife and daughter Sarah, leaving for Buckingham Palace.

King Edward VIII, afterwards Duke of Windsor, at the time of his abdication: 'I feel bound to place my personal loyalty to him upon the highest plane.'

was hissed into silence. Had there been any chance of Churchill returning to power—and the tide of his popularity had actually been coming round again—then it would have been effectively lost in this crisis. In some vague way it was felt that he had been disloyal.

Warnings of a Lone Voice

For the rest, his gloomy thunderings against the rising power of Germany were not very popular. There was much relief when Mr Baldwin was able to point out that all Churchill's figures on the expanding Nazi airforce were quite wrong; and when six months later Mr Baldwin disarmingly admitted that it was he himself who had been misled, this did not have the effect of making people remember that Churchill had been right. It was felt instead that Mr Baldwin had been very honest and straightforward in admitting his mistake. Through most of these ten years Churchill stood almost alone in his campaign for rearmament, and not even Hitler's march into the Rhineland in 1936, nor Mussolini's conquest of Abyssinia, nor the Japanese advance in Manchuria, nor even the Nazi annexation of Austria brought many people to his side. A programme of expanding the armed services was indeed begun, but it was small, tepid, and slowed down by an immense foreboding that bombing and poison gas would mean the end of civilisation anyway.

There was one more act of delusion to be committed, the last and the greatest in this decade of delusions, and when it came at Munich, Churchill made a singularly fateful speech, perhaps one of the most statesmanlike speeches he ever delivered. We had sustained, he said, 'a total and unmitigated defeat', France even more than Britain. Czechoslovakia might really have done better if she had been left to negotiate with Germany by herself; she could scarcely have had worse terms.

There was no possibility of friendship with Germany, he continued. The only hope now was for Britain to start rearming, especially in the air, on a scale which had never been attempted before. He concluded:

March, 1938: Hitler enters Austria.

Chamberlain arrives with the Munich Agreement,
30 September 1938.

On the brink of war: Churchill and Eden on their way
to Parliament.

'I do not grudge our loyal, brave people, who were ready to do their duty
no matter what the cost, who never flinched under the strain of last week—I
do not grudge them the natural, spontaneous outburst of joy and relief when
they learned that the hard ordeal would no longer be required of them at the
moment; but they should know the truth. They should know that there has
been gross neglect and deficiency in our defences; they should know that we
have sustained a defeat without a war, the consequences of which will travel
far with us along our road; they should know that we have passed an awful
milestone in our history, when the whole equilibrium of Europe has been de-
ranged . . . And do not suppose that this is the end. This is only the beginning
of the reckoning. This is only the first sip, the first foretaste of a bitter cup which
will be proffered to us year by year unless by a supreme recovery of moral health
and martial vigour, we arise again and take our stand for freedom, as in the
olden time.'

There remained still eleven months of peace. Within this period, stage by
stage, each one of Churchill's warnings was fulfilled. In March 1939 the last of

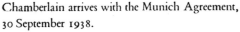

March 1939: Hitler appearing at the window of Hradčany Castle, Prague.

Czechoslovakia was gobbled up. During Easter in the following month Mussolini seized Albania. Then having signed a non-aggression pact with Russia, Hitler advanced to the conquest of Poland on 1st September. On 3rd September Britain and France declared war. That same day, under the awful pressure of the crisis, Chamberlain turned back to the man who had predicted it from the beginning: he invited Churchill into his War Cabinet as First Lord of the Admiralty.

First Lord again

The new Minister was applauded in the House at a special session that Sunday morning. Then he went back to his old rooms in Whitehall and got out the same maps which he had used when he ordered the fleet into action precisely twenty-five years before. A signal was sent out to all naval ships and shore establishments: 'Winston is back.'

Churchill was in his sixty-sixth year when he came to the Admiralty in 1939, and he was over seventy when the war ended six years later in the summer of 1945. By that time Roosevelt, Mussolini and Hitler were dead, and Stalin himself, the only other great figure of the time, had very few years to live.

Churchill was older than any of them: four years older than Stalin, eight years older than Roosevelt, nine years older than Mussolini and a good fifteen years older than Hitler. There was another important aspect that set him apart from the others: he alone among these contemporary friends and enemies was not in office when the war began. In every case the others had already been in power for a long time in 1939, they had their own nominees in all the high offices, they were the commanders-in-chief of their armed forces, and each of them had a strong system of government under his direct control.

Churchill had to create this position for himself in great haste and in time of war; and he had to do it in such a way that he never absolutely over-rode the voice of Parliament. In effect, with the consent of the House of Commons, he did become a dictator and he was given powers with which he would never have been entrusted for two minutes at any other time. 'Had it not been for the resumption of the war,' Bernard Shaw remarked, 'Churchill would not have had a dog's chance of crowning his parliamentary career as Prime Minister.' This was perfectly true; but it was also true that everyone was delighted that it should be so—just as long as the crisis lasted.

So it is against this background of power taken up very quickly, very completely and very unexpectedly towards the end of a long parliamentary career that one has to consider these six astonishing years in Churchill's life.

The prelude at the Admiralty lasted just eight months, from September 1939 to May 1940. This was almost exactly the period of the cold war, and Churchill as First Lord was fortunate not only in the fact that the Navy was the only really effective fighting force at the time, but that it was also in action. Then too both he and the British love the sea, and from the very beginning he had some tragic and wonderful things to report. There was the first U-boat strike at the liner *Athenia* off the west coast of Ireland, a few days after the hostilities had begun,

The First Lord of the Admiralty being piped aboard the battle-scarred *Exeter* at Plymouth.

and many other frightful sinkings followed very rapidly. But then there was the Battle of the River Plate (so like the Battle of the Falkland Islands in the First World War), when the cruisers *Exeter* and *Ajax* ran down the *Graf Spee* and forced her to scuttle in South American waters. 'In a cold dark winter,' Churchill said, 'it has warmed the cockles of our hearts.' Then, again, when the destroyer *Cossack* steamed into the Norwegian fjords and in a piratical fashion plucked 299 British prisoners off the German steamer *Altmark,* it really began to seem that we had arisen, as Churchill had urged us to do at the time of Munich, and had taken 'our stand for freedom, as in the olden time'.

It was this atmosphere of determined risk and exhilaration surrounding Churchill which swept him into the Prime Ministership when, within the next few weeks, the abortive Norwegian campaign collapsed and the German panzer onslaught fell on the Low Countries and France. Within a matter of

The Cabinet Room in 10 Downing Street. A headline in *The Times* of 11 May 1940. 'Thus, then, on the night of the 10th of May, at the outset of this mighty battle, I acquired the chief power in the State. . . . I was sure I should not fail.'

hours every hope was dissipated in disaster. Leopold Amery had flung Cromwell's words across the House at Chamberlain: 'Depart, I say, and let us have done with you. In the name of God, go.' Perhaps it was Chamberlain's absurd cry of a few days before, 'Hitler missed the bus', which set the blaze alight. On 10th May, when the Germans were streaming into France in the most spectacular land offensive of modern times, he gave in. On Chamberlain's advice, the King sent for Churchill that night, and asked him to form a government.

Prime Minister

'I felt,' he wrote later, 'as if I were walking with Destiny, and that all my past life had been but a preparation for this hour and for this trial.'

In the fifteen years that have elapsed since then, the words of Churchill's great speeches have rumbled so often in our ears that we tend to remember them as we remember some epic poem, some passage from a classic tragedy that we were asked to learn at school. At first they seem lost, but someone has only to start us off and the words come back with their familiar rhythm, the scene rises again, the mood of the time and the exaltation, and no matter how often the phrases are repeated it is still sometimes difficult to refrain from tears.

It was in his first address to the House as Prime Minister that he said:

'I would say to the House as I have said to those who have joined this Government: "I have nothing to offer but blood, toil, tears and sweat." We have before us an ordeal of the most grievous kind. We have before us many, many long months of struggle and of suffering. You ask, what is our policy?

I will say: It is to wage war by sea, land and air, with all our might and with all the strength that God can give us; to wage war against a monstrous tyranny, never surpassed in the dark, lamentable catalogue of human crime. That is our policy. You ask, what is our aim? I can answer in one word: it is victory, victory at all costs, victory in spite of all terror, victory however long and hard the road may be . . .'

It was in the speech on the evacuation of Dunkirk which followed with such bewildering rapidity barely three weeks later that he said: 'Even though large tracts of Europe and many old and famous States have fallen or may fall into the grip of the Gestapo and all the odious apparatus of Nazi rule, we shall not flag or fail, we shall go on to the end, we shall fight in France, and we shall fight on the seas and oceans, we shall fight with growing confidence and growing strength in the air, we shall defend our island whatever the cost may be, we shall fight on the beaches, we shall fight on the landing-grounds, we shall fight in the fields and in the streets, we shall fight in the hills; we shall never surrender.'

It was the most dangerous moment in the country's history, but such words had hardly been heard in England since Shakespeare's time; and, in fact, in the

October 1941: the War Cabinet in the garden of 10 Downing Street. *Seated:* Sir John Anderson, Churchill, Attlee, Eden; *standing:* Greenwood, Bevin, Beaverbrook, Sir Kingsley Wood.

cigarettes had been mechanically consumed. Amid the smoke he saw a peroration, which would cut deep into the hearts of a crowd; a high thought, a fine simile, expressed in that correct diction which is comprehensible even to the most illiterate, and appeals to the most simple; something to lift their minds from the material cares of life and to awake sentiment. His ideas began to take the form of words, to group themselves into sentences; he murmured to himself; the rhythm of his own language swayed him; instinctively he alliterated. Ideas succeeded one another as a stream flows swiftly by and the light changes on its waters. He seized a piece of paper and began hurriedly to pencil notes. That was a point; could not tautology accentuate it? He scribbled down a rough sentence, scratched it out, polished it, and wrote it in again. The sound would please their ears, the sense improve and stimulate their minds. What a game it was! His brain contained the cards he had to play, the world the stakes he played for.

Fifty years earlier, before he had ever made a speech, he wrote in *Savrola*, this prescription for great oratory.

years that followed they became everybody's words in every democracy and perhaps did as much to bring about Hitler's defeat as any other weapon. Under this leader there was no alternative, indeed there was no wish to do anything but fight on.

The events of the war have been so often chronicled, notably by Churchill himself, that there is no need here to do more than list some of the main happenings as an *aide memoire* in tracing the Prime Minister's activities.

Nineteen-forty was the year of disaster. Europe fell in June, and England was just able to ward off the German air attack that followed in the autumn. The one bright aspect of the year was General Wavell's offensive against the Italian Army in the Western Desert of Egypt.

In 1941 the sides finally lined up against one another. In June Hitler launched his offensive on Russia, and in December Japan brought America into the war with the attack on Pearl Harbour. This was another year of defeat for the Allies, especially Britain, who was driven out of Greece

Broadcasting to a world at war.

and Crete and whose forces everywhere fell back before the Japanese in the Far East.

The year 1942 was the turning point. The Russians held at Stalingrad, the British decimated the Axis army in the desert at El Alamein, and the Americans entered the war in North Africa.

Nineteen-forty-three was very largely a year of muddle and dissension. All Africa was cleared of the enemy, but thereafter the Mediterranean campaign bogged down in the Italian peninsula, and in the Far East the Japanese were nowhere seriously dislodged. The only notable victories of the west were in the quashing of the German U-boats and in the increasingly heavy air-raids on Germany. Russia, struggling alone against 240 German divisions, called again and again for the British and the Americans to open up a second front, but they were not ready.

Nineteen-forty-four was the decisive year: the Normandy landing in June, the reconquest of France, the Russian advance from the east, and the continuous bombardment of Germany from the air. The Germans' last hope—the flying bomb and the rocket—arrived too late to be effective.

Nineteen-forty-five was the year of victory in war and defeat in peace; the capture of Berlin and the death of Hitler came in May, the mass surrender in Italy and the death of Mussolini a few days earlier. By the time the first atomic bombs were launched on Japan

1940: 'Business as usual.' London during the 'Blitz.

1940: In the garden of 10 Downing Street, with five French boys escaped from Occupied France.

1941: Amid the ruins of the House of Commons. 'The Chamber must be rebuilt exactly as it was,' he ordered.

(June 20 40)   (Say 4000)

Secret Session.   House of Commons.

My reliance on it as an instrument for waging
                                                    war.

More active and direct part for its Members
  L.D.V.

All this in accordance with past history.

This S.S. a model of discretion.

My view always Govt. strengthened by S.S.

~~Quite ready to have others~~

Agree with idea S.S. shd be quite a normal part
  of our procedure,
        not associated with any crisis.

Relief to be able to talk without enemy reading.

Quite ready to have other S.Ss.,
        especially on precise subjects.

But I hope not press Ministers engaged in
  conduct of war too hard.
                    this week !
  ↙ refreshed by
  Mood of the House.
        Cool and robust.

Speeches most informative.   confidence & any
  Difficult to betray any secrets disclosed
                        today.

8

Moore-Brab (Wallesey)   Praise.

He was sorry I mentioned expert advisers
  favoured fighting on.

Politicians and Generals, -

In last war and this.
  Noel Baker — Derby
Not put too much on the politicians:
  even they may err.
  Noel Baker. Derby.

Goering.   How do you class him?
  He was an airman turned politician.

I like him better as an airman.
  Not very much anyway.

Moore-Brab tells us of his wonderful brain,
  and the vast dictatorial powers and plans

Anyhow he did not produce the best pilots
  or the best machines,
    or perhaps, as we may see presently,
        the best Science.

M.B. said 250 nights in the year
  when no defence against night bombing.

~~I hope it is not so~~

This is one of those things you can only tell
  by finding out.

9

Two sheets from Churchill's bundle of notes for his speech in secret session, on 20 June 1940, with his pencilled corrections.

the Chinese Communist Party was established in China and the Soviet armies had overrun Eastern Europe.

This universal struggle was wholly unlike the First World War. That war was static; this was intensely mobile, ranging all over the globe and the surrounding sky; the trenches barely existed. In the last resort this was not a war of men but of weapons. Fewer and fewer men were needed at the actual striking point, until in the end, it required only one man to pull the lever that dropped the atomic bomb on Hiroshima. Thus this Second World War was really a struggle to determine which side had the better inventions, and the greater means of mass-producing them; and so, from the very beginning, it was not a war which was led by generals at the front; it was controlled by politicians at home. They and they alone had the means to build the factories and organise the man-power.

It was Churchill's major contribution to the Prime Ministership that he grasped this situation from the beginning. His first act was to bring the Labour leaders in and create a small war council of just five members. This was a repetition of Lloyd George's war council in the First World War, but now

Portrait bust made in 1942 by
Clare Sheridan, Churchill's cousin.

Churchill went a step further, he created a Ministry of Defence with himself at
the head of it. In effect this was nothing less than a Supreme Headquarters. The
commanders in the field no longer reported only to their service ministers, or to
the chiefs-of-staff, but directly to Churchill himself as well; and directly from
him they often received their instructions. He acted of course, with the consent
of Parliament and with the advice of the chiefs-of-staff and others. Nevertheless
by this new arrangement he became the effective Commander-in-Chief of the
three services in the day-to-day conduct of the war. It is astonishing to see in his
war memoirs how closely he kept his hand upon events, sometimes even in-
structing a commander down to the disposition of divisions and brigades.

On the other hand, he divested himself almost entirely of domestic affairs.
These were turned over to others, chiefly Ernest Bevin, Attlee, Anderson and
Woolton, who in turn were assisted by a team of administrators and business-
men, all of whom were very ready to accept the Prime Minister's over-all
control.

Having thus fixed his power at home, Churchill turned to the outward
scene, and at once concentrated upon the only issue that really mattered: the

organisation of allies and supplies. He saw that England alone had not a hope of winning the war and only a slender chance of survival unless help was obtained from outside; and for the rest of the war, from Dunkirk onwards, he devoted all his chief efforts to the getting of this outside help. He journeys tirelessly from America to Russia, to the Mediterranean and back again, with this one object in view—to bring the allies in line, to borrow and exchange weapons and forces, to bend everybody's minds to the great central aim of the liberation of Europe. He becomes in fact the great persuader, and in almost every case his real victories are not the military events which are known to everybody but those he has achieved in private months beforehand by his persuasion at the conference table.

The Great Persuader

Churchill never asked for any applause for the agony of his long conversations with Stalin, with the Americans, with de Gaulle and the other exiled leaders in London, with Chiang Kai-shek and the Dominion Prime Ministers; for the wearisome journeys and conferences; for the endless correspondence and the telephonings. He may even have enjoyed some of these experiences at times (except perhaps for his association with de Gaulle: 'We all have our crosses to bear,' he once remarked. 'Mine is the Cross of Lorraine.') But whether he enjoyed them or not he never faltered in this matter. He put up with the insults of the Russians, the occasional frets of the Minor Powers, and he accepted the not always congenial role of playing second fiddle to the Americans. The constant nagging he received both from Russia and from critics in England on the delay in opening the second front—a delay that was entirely justified—cannot have been very easy to bear.

Compared to these exhausting dealings, the physical dangers of the war and the leadership of the country at home were a release and a positive joy. He was always stimulated by danger, and politically he was always at his best in a crisis. Now at last the direction was clear, and for the first time in his life he had complete control. There would be no more Gallipolis, no more Admiral Fishers and Lord Kitcheners to hold him back.

It will be seen then that the list of military events published above is not altogether a reliable guide to Churchill's personal activities during the war. In 1940, when everyone else is at the bottom, he is at the top. Dunkirk is not a defeat, it is a wonderful challenge. On taking over the Prime Ministership, he was conscious, he said, 'of a profound sense of relief'.

In June 1940 there was still something to be saved from the debacle in France: Paris had fallen but Reynaud was still Prime Minister. The French fleet was still intact. A new French government could still be set up on North Africa, and there was still a considerable French Army in Syria. All these were very considerable factors.

Three times Churchill flew to France to see Reynaud, and then he came out with a perfectly staggering offer: Britain and France should combine themselves into a union. There should be a joint parliament, the populations of both

Churchill's 69th birthday, during the 'Big Three' Conference at Teheran, 30 November 1943: 'This was a memorable occasion in my life. On my right sat the President of the United States, on my left the master of Russia.'

countries should enjoy citizenship, and there should be a joint command of the war. Because this offer came too late to bolster French morale it has been very largely forgotten in the years since then, but there is no reason whatever to doubt its sincerity, and it was in fact one of the most remarkable propositions in all European history, a gesture that makes the post-war fumblings towards a United States of Europe seem a little pallid.

Churchill was setting out once more to see Reynaud in Bordeaux when the news arrived of the French surrender. Returning to London, he committed himself to perhaps the bravest if not the wisest decision of his whole political career: he ordered the bombardment of the French fleet in Oran to prevent its defection to the Germans. At the same time he entered into the long turning tunnel of his negotiations with de Gaulle, and it is one of the wonders of this age that the two men with their nations behind them should have emerged into the sunlight again as firm allies in the liberation of Paris four years later.

For the moment, however, in the summer of 1940 Churchill was obliged to turn urgently to America. No doubt he was greatly helped by his new friend-ship with Roosevelt, and by the moving spectacle that Britain presented just then under the falling bombs, but the arrangements he made in Washington that year must certainly be accounted as a major British victory in the war. Fifty American destroyers were handed over to the British fleet, and the Ame-ricans began to patrol their own ships bound across the Atlantic for England. Lease-Lend was put through, and the two leaders, meeting at sea, 'in some lonely bay or other', drew up the Atlantic Charter, which proclaimed a doc-trine of freedom to the world. Although the Atlantic Charter created more enthusiasm among politicians than among the public, and a cynic might argue that there is hardly one of its provisions which has not since been violated, it did at the time create a certain sense of reassurance. It fixed, in however tenuous a way, some sort of spiritual aim before the two countries to match the death-and-glory creed of the Nazis; and in all the difficulties of the succeeding negotia-tions between the British and the Americans it made a bond that nobody wanted to untie. It demonstrated that in our instincts at least we were the same, however we might differ in our methods.

But there was another matter which was absolutely vital to Britain, and which might well have gone wrong had Churchill not exerted himself. When the United States came into the war in December 1941 there was a very strong case for her to turn the full weight of her counter-attack upon Japan, while England was left to fend for herself in Europe. From Churchill's point of view this would have been disastrous, and he countered it in the only possible way. He declared war on Japan, as he had promised he would, 'within the hour', and went directly to Washington. On arrival he pledged his word—and Roosevelt said he wanted nothing more than his word—that directly Germany had been de-feated Britain would turn all her energies into the attack on Japan. Roosevelt in reply agreed that Germany should be treated as Number One enemy, and Japan as Number Two; and the Americans landed in North Africa later in the year.

There remained one other major issue between the United States and Britain which came up towards the end of the war, and in this Churchill did not have his way. In 1944 he wished to abandon the attack on the south of France and instead push through the Balkans to the relief of Czechoslovakia and Vienna. Once again here he was thinking ahead and upon lines which the Americans did not care for very much and which the Russians absolutely hated. Roosevelt in those days saw no evil in the Russian advance across Europe—it was bad faith to suspect them—and Churchill was not in a position to press the point. In any event, we were all engulfed at the time in the joy of winning the war at last, and Prague and Vienna went down the Russian gullet without a murmur from the West. The consequences followed later and belong to the period immediately after the war.

With Russia Churchill's relations were more simple than they were with the

'Winterton's Nightmare.' In May 1942, Parliament discussed whether the war should be run by the Chiefs of Staff under the Minister of Defence (Churchill) or by one man (Churchill). Lord Winterton declared: 'The latter state exists already.'

Americans, perhaps for the very reason that they were so much more difficult. Churchill made no attempt whatever to deny his past hatred of the Bolsheviks. His thesis was very direct: anyone who strikes Hitler is for the time being my friend, and he remarked pleasantly in private, 'If Hitler invaded Hell I would make at least a favourable reference to the Devil in the House of Commons.' And off he went to Moscow to see what he could do with Stalin. Of all Churchill's protagonists and antagonists in the war, Stalin stands out quite clearly as the ablest, the most clear-headed, and the most determined. He was ruder than Churchill, much more ruthless and just as tough, and like Churchill

At General Eisenhower's headquarters
in Algiers, June 1943, discussing plans
for the invasion of Italy. Gathered around
Churchill: Eden, General Brooke,
Air Chief Marshal Tedder, Admiral
Cunningham, and Generals Alexander,
Marshall, Eisenhower and Montgomery.

INVASION SIGNAL

READY—STEADY— · · ·

On the eve of the 'Second Front': the world awaiting the signal for 'Operation Overlord'.

he knew exactly what he wanted. He wanted arms and he wanted a second front.

Churchill saw Stalin five times in all—on two visits to Moscow and then at the conferences at Teheran and Yalta and Potsdam and although Stalin was kept waiting a full three years for the second front he had his way in nearly everything else.

There was one other main field in which Churchill was obliged to exert his powers of persuasion, and that was at home in the House of Commons. He was seriously challenged on two occasions in 1942. He had been for a month in Canada and the United States that winter, and when he came back in January he found that the House was restless and angry, not only over his long absence but at the way the war was going. The *Prince of Wales*, the very battleship in which the Prime Minister had first sailed to meet the President, had been bombed and sunk by the Japanese with apparent ease. Singapore was falling, together with Malaya and Burma. There was still no sign whatever of a second front, and the news from the desert merely seemed to indicate that our tanks were much inferior to the German. In Whitehall itself there was still another matter for discontent: it was felt that Stafford Cripps, the one man who might have been a serious rival to Churchill, was being deliberately kept out of office.

Churchill without much trouble survived this squall, and soon afterwards went some way towards meeting his critics by bringing Stafford Cripps into the War Cabinet as Lord Privy Seal and Leader of the House. But by midsummer a much more serious situation had developed. In the Western Desert the British Army was driven out of Cyrenaica, and on 20th June Tobruk fell with the loss of 25,000 men who were taken prisoner. In the Far East nothing of the British Empire remained.

Sir John Wardlaw-Milne tabled the following motion of censure: 'That the House, while paying tribute to the heroism and endurance of the Forces of the Crown in circumstances of exceptional difficulty, has no confidence in the central direction of the war.' His seconder was Admiral of the Fleet Sir Roger Keyes, Churchill's old ally from the days of the Dardanelles. The debate that followed was perhaps chiefly interesting for the fact that Mr Aneurin Bevan emerged as the most vehement of the Government's critics, while none could outdo Mr William Gallagher, the Communist, in his support of Churchill.

There had been at this time three years of war, pretty nearly all of it unsuccessful, and the debate was not unnaturally an expression of the general ennui and discontent. Apart from the larger defeats there were smaller set-backs—such as the escape of the German battleships *Gneisenau* and *Scharnhorst* up the English Channel—which particularly caused dismay and made people feel that the war was going on forever. This was the low point in Britain, and there was now one more burden added to the blood, toil, tears and sweat: monotony. Churchill could not reveal that Roosevelt had spontaneously offered to make good all the losses of material in the desert, and that the North African landing was even then getting under way. It was surprising in these circumstances that the motion was rejected by an overwhelming majority of 475 votes against 25.

After this criticism of Churchill died away, and his fortunes rose again with the steadily improving news from the fighting front. For the most part now he had only pleasant things to announce to the House, none pleasanter perhaps than the message he received from General Alexander early in 1943: 'Sir, the orders you gave me on 15th August 1942 have been fulfilled. His Majesty's enemies together with their impedimenta, have been completely eliminated from Egypt, Cyrenaica, Libya and Tripolitania. I now await your further instructions.'

From the beginning the British had been almost alone in the desert, and this was entirely a British success. It was also the last time the British and the Dominions had to march alone, for Churchill's chain of allies round the world was now complete. From this point onwards the war rolled on inevitably to its conclusion.

June 1940. Departure from Europe: Allied troops waiting to be evacuated from the Dunkirk beaches.

June 1944. Return to Europe: unloading at 'Mulberry Beach'.

D-Day, 1944: Allied troops landing in Normandy.

Through these years Churchill's life at home—whether at Chequers in the country, at 10 Downing Street, or in the underground annexe which was built at Storey's Gate—ceased to be a private life at all. He woke at eight, and the night's dispatches were at once brought to him in bed. For a couple of hours then he read and dictated to his secretaries. He covered a fantastic range of subjects, and his memoranda, thousands upon thousands of them, often beginning with the famous apostrophe 'Pray . . . do this or that,' flowed out in a constant stream through his two chief aides, General Ismay and Sir Edward Bridges. Midway through the morning he got up, and presently emerged in his siren suit to meet the luncheon guests. After luncheon there followed a siesta of an hour or more, and by the late afternoon he was ready for more work and the new group of guests assembling for dinner. Dinner in the country was often followed by a movie, and then towards half-past ten the business of the night began. This was when he liked to see people, and often they were kept at work until three in the morning. At these late sessions he expanded, and an endless flow of ideas was explored: 'He has at least a hundred ideas a day,' Roosevelt said 'of which four are good.' The good ones included nothing quite so spectacular as the tank which he had first conceived in 1914, but still there was 'Pluto', the pipe-line-under-the-ocean that carried petrol across the Channel to France, 'Fido', the system of dispersing fog from landing-fields, and 'Mulberry', the artificial harbour which was towed across the Channel after the D-day landing in Normandy.

His health maintained that charmed steadiness of a man who is utterly occupied, and it was not until December 1943, when he was returning from the Teheran Conference (where he had passed his sixty-ninth birthday), that he was attacked by pneumonia, the same disease which had dogged him as a very small child. No penicillin was available in 1943, and for a while it was thought that the course of the disease would be serious. It was checked, however, with sulphonamide tablets (which he took without turning a hair) and he recuperated at Marakesh. In the following year he was again attacked by pneumonia, while on a secret visit to Italy, but this illness was of short duration.

For the rest, he was followed by the same luck that had brought him through all the wars of his youth and the various plane crashes and car accidents ever since. No bomb caught him when he watched the air raids from the roof at Storey's Gate in London, or when he travelled to the front on the Continent. He was prepared to go some way in defying those who tried to protect him. When Eisenhower refused him permission to sail on D-day, he replied that he would join the complement of some British vessel over which the Supreme Commander had no control. It was only when the King announced that if Churchill was going then he would go too that Churchill desisted.

There was an immense love for Churchill in England through these days. No other figures except the King and Queen and the Queen Mother ever approached his popularity or exerted the same emotional hold upon crowds wherever he went. They knew every one of his uniforms and his hats, the siren suits, the bow tie, the shoes with the zip fasteners, the walking-stick, the watch-chain, the gloves and the keys dangling from his pocket. Nothing apparently could ever weary them of the V-sign or the cigar, and the first sounds of the grumpy reassuring voice on the radio silenced all conversation in any pub or public place. His *bons mots* were repeated without end, and it is a surprising thing that no one yet has compiled a book of the thousand stories that were woven round his name.

It was not an unblemished record. He had made many mistakes and mis-calculations. Like everyone else he had wholly underrated the Soviet fighting strength in the beginning, and his mistrust of the Russian leaders was not so great that it could prevent him from assuring the House that he was certain they would respect Poland. 'I feel that their word is their bond,' he said. In Greece he had allowed a dangerous situation to develop to the point of civil war, and it was only settled when he himself appeared upon the scene; and his handling of the Dominions, notably India and Australia, had not always been successful. At home, too, many people thought, somewhat unfairly, that he had shown only the most tepid interest in the reconstruction of the country after the war.

August 1944: King George VI with some of his principal ministers.

But all this was nothing compared to the intense gratitude which the country felt towards him. He had not only led them to the promised victory: he had conferred upon Britain a new dignity in which everyone felt he had a part.

When finally he got up in the House on 8th May 1945 to announce that there was peace in Europe, it seemed that England itself was personified in this one indomitable man. The House rose and waved their order papers at him. He moved a simple resolution which was almost identical with one which had been passed a quarter of a century before: 'That this House do now attend at the Church of St Margaret, Westminster, to give humble and reverent thanks to Almighty God for our deliverance from the threat of German domination.'

He then followed the Speaker in the procession of the members across to the church on the other side of the road.

That night a vast crowd gathered in Whitehall and looked up, cheering wildly, to the balcony where he was standing. It was Ernie Bevin who beat time for them as they sang, 'For he's a jolly good fellow,' a curiously inadequate song, with inadequate words, since for many people there, and indeed for people all over the world, the moment was almost too much to be borne.

Eleven weeks later Churchill was removed from office in one of the worst defeats the Conservatives had suffered since the beginning of the century.

In the summer of 1945 Winston Churchill was seventy. Hitler was dead. England under his leadership was delivered from fear, and for that reason if for no other, ecstatic crowds followed him wherever he went. It was only in the background that the discontent was gathering, and it was so diffuse, so much without a leader or a rallying point, that nobody was able to assess it or predict what was about to happen, perhaps least of all Churchill himself.

Victory and
Defeat

In May, soon after the defeat of Germany, Churchill expressed the very reasonable wish to his Labour colleagues in the Cabinet that they should carry on the Coalition until Japan was defeated. The Labour Party, however, was inclined to think that this was too indefinite. They were opposed to an immediate election, but at the same time nearly ten years had gone by since the Conservatives had come into the House with a dominant majority, and they believed that the Socialist programme could not be delayed much longer. Having consulted his party, Attlee proposed that a time limit of three months should be set. This was at once rejected by the Tories, mainly on the grounds that it put an impossible strain on the Prime Minister's freedom of action while he was still fighting a war. In fact, the three months' period would have just about taken us through to Japan's defeat, but nobody could have guessed this at the time. Attlee was informed that if there was to be an election then it would be held immediately. On 23rd May 1945, Churchill resigned, the date of the election was fixed at 5th July, and in the meantime a 'caretaker' government was formed to carry on the pressing business of the summer.

Churchill had never been exactly predictable, but in the campaign that followed he confounded even those friends who thought they knew him best.

Before:
Hitler and General Keitel inspecting the giant bunker of the 'Siegfried Line', in construction near Aachen.

After:
Churchill and General Montgomery inspecting the 'Dragon's Teeth' of the 'Siegfried Line', conquered near Aachen.

16 July 1945. The end in Berlin: Churchill leaving Hitler's air-raid shelter in the Chancellery. 'I went down to the bottom and saw the room in which he and his mistress had committed suicide.'

'Victory in Europe' Day, 9 May 1945. The Prime Minister surrounded by cheering crowds on his way from Downing Street to the House of Commons.

27 July 1945: Clement Richard Attlee, the new Prime Minister, waving to the cheering crowds.

A SWEEPING LABOUR VICTORY

◆

LARGE WORKING MAJORITY

MR. CHURCHILL'S RESIGNATION ACCEPTED BY THE KING

MR. ATTLEE ASKED TO FORM A GOVERNMENT

'I was immediately dismissed by the British electorate from all further conduct of their affairs.' *The Times* headlines announcing Churchill's defeat and resignation.

His prestige was so high, and his name was now so firmly identified with the political life of England, that nothing was required of him but the 'great states-man' approach: a series of formal speeches in the Augustan manner, a few good-humoured thrusts at his opponents. Instead, he chose to fight the campaign as though a general strike was raging once more in England, and as if he himself was making a desperate stand for his political existence.

In his opening speech on the radio he declared that Socialism would lead to the creation of some form of Gestapo in England. The word Gestapo had a particularly hateful meaning just then, and after this initial broadside the Prime Minister went on to attack his opponents by name: his wartime colleagues Attlee and Bevin, and more particularly Professor Laski, the Chairman of the Labour Party Executive.

To people who knew Attlee and the other Labour leaders to be honourable men who had unobtrusively supported Churchill in the war, these insinuations seemed misplaced, even an affront. What they were really concerned about was that we should not return to the unemployment and misery that had followed the First World War. Compared to the precise though drastic programme offered by the Socialists, the Conservative five-year-plan prepared by Lord Woolton appeared to be an anaemic and half-hearted thing—and in any case Churchill did not give the impression that he was over-much interested in it. His references to milk for babies and built-in cupboards for housewives sounded a little unreal—rather like some society hostess talking about bottling plums for the parish poor.

Nevertheless, with all these factors at work the actual result of the election was a staggering surprise. It was a landslide only to be compared with the victory of the Liberals over the Conservatives in 1906. Labour was in with 394 seats against 188 for the Conservatives.

For some months Churchill gave the appearance of going about his affairs as though he was too shocked and stunned to credit what had happened. He declined a high honour from the King, and angrily denounced the election as 'one of the greatest disasters that has smitten us in our long and chequered history'. No one wished to gloat over this brutal, almost unbelievable reversal of his fortunes, but it was thought now that it would be best for all concerned if the old man retired with his glory to his books and his paintings in the role of the honoured elder statesman. It had been a wonderful life, but now it was enough. No need for him to worry himself any more with trivial party debates in Whitehall. He was above all that and he needed a rest.

It was said at the beginning of this study that perhaps the real crises of Churchill's life are not those by which he is best known, but others which he resolved in private by himself; and it may be that this was just such a moment.

If there can be such a thing as an *embarras de courage* then the decisions he took now were its expression. He emerged and announced that he would not retire. He would give up neither the leadership of the Conservative Party, nor the

Two Churchills: second thoughts on the results of the General Election.

leadership of the Opposition in the House. He would not abandon any of his politics or unsay anything that he had said. In short, even though he was out of office everything was to go on exactly as it had before, and at the same hot pace. Even the golden sense of humour had returned. When someone suggested that he should make a tour of the cities of England so that they could do him honour he said: 'I refuse to be exhibited like a prize bull whose chief attraction is its past prowess.'

Before a year was out very definite proof was given that these things were not an old man's *intransigeance*. On receiving an honorary degree at Westminster College in Fulton, Missouri, on 5th March 1946, he made a speech which dotted all the i's of his wartime predictions, and added a few more. The speech, which was given under the chairmanship of President Truman, provoked an outcry at the time—here was Churchill, the professional Russian-hater, stirring up war again—but its ideas are the basis of the foreign policy of all the Western democracies today. He said:

The Iron Curtain

'From Stettin in the Baltic to Trieste in the Adriatic, an iron curtain has descended across the Continent. Behind that line lie all the capitals of the ancient states of Central and Eastern Europe. Warsaw, Berlin, Prague, Vienna, Budapest, Belgrade, Bucharest and Sofia, all these famous cities and the populations around them lie in what I must call the Soviet sphere, and are all subject in one form or another, not only to Soviet influence but to a very high, and, in many cases, increasing measure of control from Moscow ... Police governments are prevailing in nearly every case ... Except in the British Commonwealth, and in the United States, where Communism is in its infancy, the Communist parties or fifth columns constitute a growing challenge and peril to Christian civilisation. These are sombre facts for anyone to have to recite on the morrow of a victory gained by so much splendid comradeship in arms and in the cause of freedom and democracy; but we should be most unwise not to face them squarely while time remains ...'

This was long before the days of Senator McCarthy and the Korean War, before even Czechoslovakia was overrun. Up to this time nobody had thought of an iron curtain; we were still in the glow of Yalta; Truman's policy was still the policy of Roosevelt and such a thing as a Russian blockade of Berlin was unimagined.

The Round Table at the Potsdam Conference, July–August 1945, with Churchill, Eden, Attlee, Molotov, Stalin, Montgomery and others.

With President Truman, in conference at the White House, Washington.

The Yalta Conference of February 1945 has been fixed since then by many a good book and many an indignant though belated speech into a special niche: that was the conference at which we are said to have lost the peace. Roosevelt, filled with the notion that he could 'handle' Stalin, and determined not to allow British 'colonialism' to persist, gave way to the Russians at every point.

Yet in reality nothing was decided at Yalta that was not already in the making. It may be painful now to remember, but there was an overwhelming desire in the world to make terms with Russia at that time. Neither in the United States nor in Britain could Roosevelt or Churchill have carried a policy that was openly hostile to Russia even if they had wanted to. The difference between the two men was not over whether or not you befriended Russia but over the method of approach. Roosevelt claimed you would never get anywhere with Russia if you approached her with one hand—an armed hand—behind your

The Fulton Speech, 5 March 1946.

back. Churchill believed that it was unwise, all the same, to uncover yourself too much; if there were positions of advantage we could conveniently take up in our advance across Europe, then we had better have them.

Churchill's position at Yalta was one of extreme difficulty. He saw that he was being, to some extent, cold-shouldered by Roosevelt, he disliked and feared the soft approach to Russia, and he resented the President's charges of British colonialism. But there was very little he could do about all this: Roosevelt at that time was not open to persuasion. He was convinced that if he and Stalin could settle the world together, and if Britain got in the way then it was just too bad for Britain.

Moreover it was implicit in Churchill's policy that Britain and America must hang together whatever happened; and so for the time being the only line

Inspecting Spahi troops in the Court of Honour in the Invalides, Paris, before receiving the Medaille Militaire, France's highest military award.

The Place de la Bourse, Brussels, 27 February 1949. A vast crowd waiting to hear Churchill speak on European Unity.

At the Council of Europe 1949.

Addressing the Council of Europe at Strasbourg, on 11 August 1950, when he called for the creation of a European Army.

to take was to wait, like a neglected lover, for the President's wayward ardour for Russia to cool down with experience.

It is, however, demonstrably untrue that Churchill and Roosevelt fell out over this issue. From the seemingly hopeless day when Roosevelt sent a message to Churchill that whatever happened he would see Britain through, Churchill regarded the President as the best friend Britain ever had, and he never wavered in that opinion.

But when Churchill got up at Fulton with his iron-curtain speech in 1946 it was a most unpopular thing to do, and he continued to be unpopular with the Labour Party in England and with progressive thinking everywhere until the Berlin blockade and the Korean War made such unpopularity grotesque.

It was this speech, and another he made at Zurich in September of the same year, that first began to bring Churchill back into his old leadership again, at any rate as far as foreign affairs were concerned. Then in the following year he launched the European Movement at a mass meeting in the Albert Hall in London. This was the other sunnier side of the hopes with which we ended the war. Churchill pre-eminently was the man to lead the movement, and here he was pressing it forward with almost the same enthusiasm he had when he

Portrait bust made by Jacob Epstein in 1946.

General Election, 1951. Though his party is
narrowly defeated, Churchill retains his seat and is
being congratulated by his Labour opponent.

General Election, 1951: the Leader of the Opposition arrives at his London polling station to cast his vote.

gathered the allies together in time of war. He spoke again very warmly at the Congress of Europe, which opened at The Hague in May 1948, and when all was ready for the first meeting of the Council of Europe at Strasbourg in the summer of 1949 it was expected that his address—the key-speech of the meeting —would provide the impetus to send the movement on its way.

But by now a great deal had happened. In France and Italy the Communist parties had obtained a huge membership. At home in England public opinion both on the Left and the Right had hardened against the movement. To the experts—especially in the Treasury—it appeared that there could be nothing more dangerous than the pooling of the British pound with the weak currencies of Europe, in a Europe too, where taxes are seldom gathered with detachment and where the civil services had other standards than ours. Moreover, there was an election pending within the next few months.

Churchill's speech was a bitter disappointment to every enthusiast who hoped that somehow, by some chemical change in human nature, we could make something constructive of the peace.

'We must thoroughly explore all the various possibilities,' he said, 'and a committee, working coolly and without haste, should in a few months, be able to show the practical steps which would be most helpful to us.'

He added, 'To take a homely and familiar test, we may just as well see what the girl looks like before we marry her'—a phrase that made his hearers think, with reason, that the marriage was to be indefinitely postponed.

A smilar caution and sobriety seemed to have overtaken Churchill's politics at home. He still predicted that dire ruin would fall on the country so long as Labour was in power, but his attendances at the House were not very frequent, and some of the earlier Socialist measures, notably the nationalization of the mines and the Bank of England, went through with scarcely a ripple from the Conservative benches. In the election campaign that followed, in 1950, all reference to the Gestapo and the bad faith of his opponents was dropped. This time the Conservative Party did not make the mistake of going to the country on the strength of Churchill's reputation alone: they had also a social programme of their own prepared by Mr R. A. Butler and others, and although Churchill was reputed to have shown very little interest in it he at least offered no op-position.

The actual election was, as Churchill himself described it, 'positively demure', but the results were almost as startling as in 1945. The huge Labour vote was all but reversed: they had a bare majority of six, and it was patent that before long there was bound to be another election. It was clear, moreover, that far from having been diminished by his earlier defeat, Churchill was coming in with the tide. There was now no further talk of Eden replacing him as head of

On a painting holiday at Camera
Delobos, Madeira.

'St. Jean-Cap Ferrat', one of Churchill's favourite
spots on the French Riviera, where he painted this
picture in 1946.

In his study at Chartwell Manor.

the party. 'When I want to tease Anthony,' he remarked blithely one day, 'I remind him that Mr Gladstone formed his last Administration at the age of eighty-three.'

Meanwhile throughout these five years in Opposition, Churchill's private life was filled with a spate of activity which would have exhausted any ordinary man who was half his age, and with twice the time at his disposal. Five hundred acres were purchased near his home at Chartwell Manor, so that he could engage in farming, and at the same time he established his racing stable. For an owner starting so late in life the results were spectacular. Carrying Lord Randolph Churchill's old colours, chocolate and pink, Colonist II, a grey three-year-old, won at Ascot in 1949, and then in 1950 went on to a run of successes. Before he was sold, Colonist II won thirteen races for Churchill, and his prize money totalled £13,000. There was promising material, too, in another five horses that were training in the Churchill stable.

The painting continued; hundreds of unsigned and untitled pictures, which simply piled up on the walls and in the back rooms of Chartwell. With one exception none of these later paintings have ever been offered for sale, but some idea of their value can be gained by that exception. It was the 'Blue Sitting Room at Trent Park', which was auctioned for charity at Christie's in 1949. It went to the São Paulo collection for 1,250 guineas. Senhor Francisco de Assi Chateaubriand, the owner of that collection, said he would have been willing to have gone to £13,000. Churchill first entered the Royal Academy with two pictures under the name of Mr Winter, so he can hardly be said to have been accepted upon anything but his merits. Since then he has exhibited at the Academy every year, usually three or four landscapes, which can be recognized fairly easily by his passion for bold designs and very bright colour.

But these things were the relaxations of his seventies. The real work was his writing and that was enormous. There are well over a million and a half words in his six volumes on the Second World War, and for the production of this vast compilation—one can scarcely call it an ordinary book—he again assembled a team of secretaries, historians, technical experts, research workers and editorial assistants. They rolled forward through forests and prairies of wartime documents like a large reaping and binding machine, rejecting, codifying and sorting, and it is a miracle that in so short a time such a staggering quantity of material should have passed through one mind and that the final text should have come from Churchill's own hand. There were times when secretaries were working in shifts all through the night, and often eight or nine thousand words would be dictated in a single day. As a record of war, these volumes are not quite paralleled by any other work in any other language, and they have probably been read, in part at least, by a larger contemporary audience than any other book has ever had before. The syndication alone, in newspapers and magazines all over the world, reached scores of millions of people in many different languages, and the six volumes as a whole are still being sold. For the syndication

On the eve of his 74th birthday: spending a day with the Old Surrey and Burstors Hunt, near his home at Chartwell.

1954: with Mrs Pandit,
sister of the Prime Minister of
India, at Chartwell.

rights Churchill is said to have received well over a million dollars, and the total income from the work must eventually amount to a good deal more.

A notable photograph was taken of Churchill when he was in the middle of these labours. There he sits on a horse, riding crop in his hand, square black hat on his head, aged seventy-five or thereabouts, the most unauthor-like author that ever was. He was out with the Old Surrey and Burstow Hunt at the time, and this picture presents again the enigma of that apparently inexhaustible constitution. It admits of no perfect explanation. The admixture of sound British and American blood, and the background of a solid home in Victorian England, was of course a wonderful beginning. Then too he has lived a

With Marshal Tito of Yugoslavia.

With Chancellor Dr Adenauer
of Germany.

With Foreign Minister Gromyko
of the Soviet Union.

sensible life: his home and his family have always been around him. Most certainly he has been very greatly helped by his wife. Any harm that might have devolved from his late hours is more than outweighed by the regular meals and the excellent habit of taking a siesta in the afternoon.

He is never idle, and moving among interesting people and events he is never bored. He never takes holidays in the ordinary sense, but immediately directs himself upon some definite occupation like painting or brick-laying, which is in strong contrast with his work. And always he is captivated by the matter in hand. In brief, he is never a spectator: he takes part actively in every experience that comes his way, and opposition acts quite simply as a stimulant.

Yet when all this is said—and when one has taken into account the comfortable circumstances in his life, the excellent doctors, the frequent changes of scene—there still remains the mystery of his continuing energy, and one can no more explain it than one can explain the fabulous memory, the *penchant* for dressing-up in uniforms and strange hats, the slurred 's' in his speech, or his curious dislike of the noise of whistling.

It seemed to his friends that with all the slowing down of old age at seventy-seven he was still able to rise to an occasion as he had done twenty years before; and an occasion, which in its way was as important to him as anything that had passed before, did in fact present itself in 1951.

'Sir Winston Churchill.' The Court Circular of 24 April 1953, announcing that the British Prime Minister has ceased to be plain 'Mr Churchill'.

COURT CIRCULAR.

WINDSOR CASTLE

24th April, 1953.

The Prime Minister and Mrs. Churchill and His Excellency the High Commissioner for the Union of South Africa and Mrs. Geyer have arrived at the Castle.

The Right Hon. Winston Churchill, M.P., had an audience of The Queen this evening when Her Majesty conferred upon him the honour of Knighthood and invested him with the Insignia of a Knight Companion of the Most Noble Order of the Garter.

A crowd of amateur camera fans at Boston, Massachusetts.

In the autumn of that year, after barely eighteen months in office, the Labour Government fell. The gold reserves were falling again, food rationing still continued, and to many people who had once voted enthusiastically for Labour's social reforms, it seemed that all initiative in life was being lost in a welter of prohibitions and heavy taxation.

All this was immensely in Churchill's favour, and he conducted a sober and skilful campaign. Where before his personal appearance had been triumphant and his policies seemed to be unreal, the situation was almost reversed. He was listened to now more for his wisdom than for his personality and his record. It was the future and not the past prowess of the bull that counted. The country went to the polls in October and returned him with a majority of nineteen.

To Churchill, who had now been more than fifty years in Parliament, this was something more than another victory in another election. He had been brought into power, not as the result of a crisis, nor through any exceptional

Prime Minister again

In Washington again, June 1954: the Prime Minister entering the White House, followed by Foreign Ministers Anthony Eden and John Foster Dulles.

Wishing President Eisenhower 'Good-bye and good luck', after their week-end Conference at the White House, 19 June 1954.

With his successor, Sir Anthony Eden, a few months before handing over the premiership.

circumstances but because he was now the accepted leader of his party in all times, good or bad. He was no longer a dangerous man, only useful amongst storms or gales: the sailor was home from the sea.

As if by some special dispensation a remarkable improvement overtook British affairs almost from the moment when Churchill took office. The Korean War ended, and when during the summer of 1954 an armistice was arranged in Indo-China, there was less open conflict in the world than at any time since the day when Churchill first mobilised the British Grand Fleet against the Kaiser, precisely forty years before.

In the summer of 1955 Churchill's long career at the head of affairs came to an end. But his political life was not yet over, for in the election that followed a few weeks later he was returned as a private member for Woodford. He had no office in Sir Anthony Eden's government, but he remained there on the back benches, serene, revered, unrepressed, and still the greatest Parliamentarian of them all. Thus the story of this extraordinary life begins to pass into legend.

Yet it is not likely that Churchill will be best remembered for the warmth and glow of this Indian summer of his old age; nor is his mere longevity so

Retirement into Legend

The Prime Minister and his poodle on their way from Downing Street to Chartwell, for a rest.

Pet poodle 'Fluffy' and his master at Larvotto Beach, Monte Carlo.

Bidding farewell to the Queen after he entertained her to dinner for the last time as Prime Minister.

At the Boer Veteran's parade. St. Paul's Cathedral,
17 July, 1949.

remarkable as the actual timing of his life in history. His career almost exactly
spans the period from the Industrial Revolution to its ultimate conclusion in
atomic energy, from the age of privilege to the age of the mass-produced common
man, from the era of separate sovereign states to the present pattern of grand
alliances. At his birth Britain was the strongest power in the world, but it is
hardly probable that she will ever again have a separate island existence; in
some form or another she will re-join the Continent and act with allies overseas.
Through six reigns—that of Queen Victoria and her son Edward VII, and his
son George V, and his son Edward VIII, and his brother George VI, and his
daughter Queen Elizabeth II—Churchill has watched the slow and difficult
metamorphosis of the greatest empire the world has ever seen into a commonwealth of self-governing states, and it has been a process that has always found
him somewhat hanging back. He never believed that self-government was an
immediate panacea for social discontent, and he was never wholly willing to
sacrifice tradition for a political theory. His methods were very British: to fight
all changes tooth and nail, and then having won or lost, to settle a handsome
and magnanimous peace. Change has been the enemy in Churchill's life, and
he has never had anything but change; consequently he has almost always been
moving against the tide.

At the dispatch box, 25 February 1955. A water-colour made by Edward Ardizzone from the
Press Gallery of the House of Commons.

To all to whom these Presents shall come The Governor, Deputy Governor and Committee of the COMPANY OF ADVENTURERS OF ENGLAND TRADING INTO HUDSON'S BAY Send Greeting! Know ye that We by virtue of the Power and Authority to us given by The Most High and Mighty Prince CHARLES II by the Grace of God of Great Britain, France and Ireland King, Defender of the Faith by His Letters Patent bearing date the Second day of May in the Twenty-second year of His Reign do hereby constitute and appoint

SIR WINSTON LEONARD SPENCER CHURCHILL

Knight of the Most Noble Order of the Garter, Member of the Order of Merit, Member of the Order of the Companions of Honour, a Member of Parliament and One of Her Majesty's Most Honourable Privy Council to be

THE GRAND SEIGNEUR

of the said COMPANY OF ADVENTURERS OF ENGLAND TRADING INTO HUDSON'S BAY.

Given under our Common Seal at our house in London this Thirteenth day of December in the Fourth year of the Reign of Our Sovereign Lady ELIZABETH II by the Grace of God of the United Kingdom of Great Britain and Northern Ireland and of Her other Realms and Territories Queen, Head of the Commonwealth, Defender of the Faith and in the year of Our Lord One thousand nine hundred and fifty-five.

Keswick
Governor

Henry Benson
Deputy Governor

Appointed, like his great
ancestor the first
Duke of Marlborough,
Grand Seigneur of the
Hudson Bay Company.

With Field-Marshal Lord Montgomery at Hastings.

Looking out on the Atlas Mountains: on a painting holiday at Asni, Morocco.

Home again from a
private visit to New York
in May.

At the Wren Chapel, Chelsea, for the christening of the fifth child of his youngest daughter
Mary (Mrs Christopher Soames), 21 July 1959.

'I married and lived happily ever afterwards.' Sir Winston
and Lady Churchill with their son Randolph and their granddaughter
Arabella, celebrating their Golden Wedding at Nice, 1958.

It has been an engaging and sometimes baffling mixture: the slightly old-fashioned figure who is forever grappling with the future, the amateur who becomes the professional at everything he does, the aggressive individualist who is one of the most faithful servants the House of Commons ever had. Churchill loves the House of Commons. He has never at any point in his long life tried to defy its rules or override its authority.

Without question Churchill has been the most expressive Prime Minister England has ever had, not the most scholarly and perhaps not even the most eloquent, but none of his predecessors, not even Disraeli, ever combined the gifts of writing and speaking as he does. It hardly seems possible that the best of his speeches can fail to pass into English literature, though the place of his books is not yet absolutely certain. His style is a dangerous style, at its best going beyond excellence into other levels of its own, but skirting very near anti-climax at times. Where one examines some of his polished and resounding antitheses—'They are decided only to be undecided, resolved to be irresolute, adamant for drift, allpowerful for impotence'—they seem to be not much more than highly ingenious words, a massive nothingness.

But all this fades away before the tremendous scope and inspiration of his best work, the superb touches of humour and irony, and the marvellous control he exercises over his theme.

Of his gifts as a legislator and an arbitrator there can equally be no doubt. He has held every important Cabinet post except the Foreign Office, and un-numbered acts passed by Parliament in the last fifty years have flowed either directly or indirectly from his brain. Probably there will always be controversy over his talents as a strategist in war, though he is nearly always to be found on the winning side when the fog has cleared away; and certainly in political fore-sight and in negotiation with the foreign powers Britain has produced few, if any, leaders with whom he can be compared.

As an archetype of his own times he must be regarded at least as the greatest Briton since Wellington; and he remains in addition, with all his warmth, his charm and his infectious gusto, very much as G. W. Steevens described him nearly sixty years ago: 'The youngest man in Europe'.

Yet in the end the chances are that all these qualities of his will be superseded in memory by a quite different and much more intangible thing. For this generation of Englishmen at least, and possibly for many others to come, it will always be remembered that at the lowest moment of the country's history, when everything appeared to be lost, he somehow succeeded in raising Britain's name to a height which it had seldom, if ever, occupied before.

Churchill wrote his own epitaph at that time. It is doubtful if ever again we shall hear the words 'We shall never surrender' without recalling the voice, the adamantine ring, the utter courage, and the dignity it seemed to confer on all decent men in every age and everywhere.

CHRONOLOGY

1874 Winston Spencer Churchill, elder son of Lord Randolph Churchill and Lady Churchill (*née* Jennie Jerome), is born at Blenheim Palace on 30 November.

1888 He enters Harrow School in the lowest form.

1892 He wins the Public Schools' Fencing Competition. During a stay at Bournemouth he falls thirty feet from a tree and after being unconscious for three days makes a slow recovery.

1893 Churchill is sent to a 'crammer' in London for six months in order to pass the entrance examination for Sandhurst. He succeeds at the third attempt and enters the cavalry.

1894 He passes out of Sandhurst eighth in order of merit out of one hundred and fifty.

1895 On 24 January his father dies. In March, Churchill is gazetted to the Fourth Hussars. He obtains permission to visit the Spanish Army in action against a rebellion in Cuba. On his twenty-first birthday he is under fire for the first time. He sends articles to the *Daily Graphic* in London.

1896-97 Churchill serves as a Second-Lieutenant in India. At first stationed in Bangalore, he manages to see service with the Malakand Field Force on the Northwest Frontier. He sends dispatches to the *Daily Telegraph*.

1898 Churchill joins Kitchener's Army in Egypt, having arranged to supply a series of dispatches to the London *Morning Post.* He takes part in the charge of the Twenty-first Lancers at the Battle of Omdurman. Publication of his first book, *The Malakand Field Force.*

1899 Churchill returns to India, plays in the winning team in a polo tournament at Meerut. He resigns his commission in order to enter politics in England. Having made his first political speech at a Conservative fete at Bath, he contests the Oldham by-election but loses by fifteen hundred votes. October: He sets out for the Boer War as correspondent of the *Morning Post.* Captured two weeks after his arrival he makes a daring escape from Pretoria into Portuguese East Africa. He temporarily rejoins the Army, and takes part in the relief of Ladysmith. Publication of *The River War*, an account of the reconquest of the Sudan, and of his only novel, *Savrola.*

1900 After entering Pretoria with the victorious army, Churchill returns to England. He is elected Conservative Member for Oldham in the 'Khaki Election' with a slender majority and goes to the United States on a lecture tour. Publication of *London to Ladysmith* and *Ian Hamilton's March*, his two books on the South African War.

1901 Churchill takes his seat in the House of Commons for the first time and makes his maiden speech (18 February).

1904 After increasing friction and disagreement with the Balfour Government over Joseph Chamberlain's policy of Protection, Churchill crosses the Floor of the House to join the Liberal Party.

1906 Churchill is elected Liberal Member for North-west Manchester with a majority of thirteen hundred in the General Election. He is given his first political office as Under-Secretary of State for the Colonies

in Campbell-Bannerman's Ministry. Publication of his biography of his father, *Lord Randolph Churchill.*

1907 He is sworn in as a Privy Councillor; tours East Africa.

1908 Churchill enters Asquith's Cabinet as President of the Board of Trade. Defeated in by-election at Oldham he becomes Member for Dundee. He marries Miss Clementine Hozier on 12 September. Publication of *My African Journey.*

1909 Churchill takes a prominent part in the Government's progressive social legislation programme: establishment of trade boards, labour exchanges, unemployment and sickness insurance, etc. He becomes a champion for Lloyd George's controversial 'People's Budget' in the fight against the veto of the House of Lords. Birth of his first daughter, Diana, on 11 July. Publication of *The People's Rights.*

1910 Churchill is re-elected Liberal Member for Dundee in both General Elections of this year and is appointed Home Secretary. He sends a force of metropolitan police to maintain order during a Welsh mining strike ('Tonypandy Incident').

1911 Churchill causes considerable surprise by appearing at the 'Battle of Sydney Street'. October: He becomes First Lord of the Admiralty. Birth of his only son, Randolph on 28 May.

1912-14 Churchill modernizes the Navy, becomes interested in aviation, sets up the Royal Naval Flying Corps, and has an early version of the tank constructed ('Winston's Folly').

1914 July: Churchill prevents the dispersal of the Home Fleet after the annual exercises in July. On 1-2 August, on his own initiative, he orders the mobilization of the Fleet and sends the North Sea Squadrons to their battle stations. October: He organizes and accompanies the Antwerp Expedition. November: He recalls Lord Fisher as First Sea Lord. Birth of his second daughter, Sarah, on 7 October.

1915 February: Churchill forms Land Ships Committee at the Admiralty to expedite production of tanks. After the failure of the Dardanelles Expedition, Churchill is obliged to leave the Admiralty and accepts office as Chancellor of the Duchy of Lancaster in the Coalition Government (May). On 11 November he resigns from the Cabinet to serve in France, and is given command of a battalion of the Royal Scots Fusiliers.

1916 After six months' service in the trenches, Churchill's Battalion is absorbed and he returns to civilian life.

1917 Churchill appointed Minister of Munitions in Lloyd George's Ministry, and presses forward production of the new tanks.

1918 Churchill is re-elected Liberal Member for Dundee in the General Election. Becomes Secretary of State for War and for Air. He appeals for volunteer troops to cover withdrawal of British troops from Russia. Birth of his third daughter, Marigold Frances, on 15 November (died 23 August 1921).

1919 During a flying outing, Churchill crashes his aircraft at Croydon, but escapes unhurt. He has a painting exhibited at the Royal Society of Portrait Painters' Exhibition.

1921 Churchill becomes Colonial Secretary, is a member of the Cabinet Committee who negotiate a treaty with the leaders of the Irish Rebellion. At the Cairo Conference Churchill negotiates a Middle East settlement, with T. E. Lawrence as his adviser.

1922 Churchill stands as a National Liberal for Dundee at the General Election—he is defeated by one thousand two hundred votes. He is made a Companion of Honour. Birth of his fourth daughter, Mary, on 15 September.

1923 He contests a by-election at Leicester West as a National Liberal and is defeated by four thousand votes. First volume of *The World Crisis* published. (Sixth and last volume published in 1931.)

1924 Churchill is again defeated at a Westminster by-election, this time by forty-three votes. In the October General Election he is elected Constitutionalist Member for Epping with a large majority, and becomes Chancellor of the Exchequer in Baldwin's Ministry. He rejoins the Conservative Party.

1925 Churchill's first Budget: he announces a return to the gold standard to strengthen the pound and an insurance scheme to cover widows and orphans.

1926 During the General Strike, Churchill edits the *British Gazette* published by the Government, which reaches a circulation of over two million with its eighth and last issue.

1927 Churchill visits Mussolini in Rome.

1928 Churchill is invited to become member of Amalgamated Union of Building Trades Workers.

1929 Re-elected Conservative Member for Epping in General Election. Visits Canada and at the end of the year becomes Rector of Edinburgh University and Chancellor of Bristol University.

1930 Churchill quarrels with Baldwin over his Indian policy. Publication of *My Early Life*, his autobiography.

1931 In January resigns from the Conservative 'Shadow Cabinet' on the India issue. He is re-elected Conservative Member for Epping with a huge majority, goes to the United States on a lecture tour and in December is knocked down by a taxi in New York.

1932 Publication of *Thoughts and Adventures*.

1933 In August, Churchill makes a speech warning of German rearmament. Publication of first volume of *Marlborough, His Life and Times*. (Fourth and last volume published in 1938.)

1934 In the debate on Air Estimates in March, Churchill urges stronger Air Defences. He charges Hoare and Derby with breach of privilege as members of the Select Committee on Indian Constitutional Reform, but the charge is dismissed in June. November: He warns the House of Commons that Germany will reach parity in air strength in 1935.

1935 Churchill joins the Committee of Imperial Defence on Air Defence Research and is re-elected Conservative Member for Epping with a large majority. Germany makes a diplomatic protest over an article by Churchill in the *Strand Magazine* in which he warns against Hitler's intentions.

1936 November: Churchill demands a Parliamentary Inquiry into the state of the nation's defences and attacks the policy of the Government. December: He is summoned to advise King Edward VIII during the Abdication crisis.

1937 Churchill meets Ribbentrop, warns him against underrating England. Publication of *Great Contemporaries*.

1938 Churchill goes to Paris in March for a series of meetings with French military and political leaders. He protests against the renunciation of British rights in Southern Irish ports. October: Churchill describes the Munich Agreement as 'a defeat without a war'.

1939 July: Churchill visits the French Rhine front. On 3 September with the outbreak of war, he is a member of the War Cabinet as First Lord of the Admiralty in the Chamberlain Government. He makes his first war broadcast on 1 October.

1940 Churchill becomes President of the Military Co-ordination Committee in April, defends the Government's conduct of the war in a debate which leads to Chamberlain's resignation. Summoned by the King, he becomes Prime Minister and Minister of Defence on 11 May, and forms a National Coalition Government which includes the Labour and Liberal Parties. He makes his 'blood, toil, tears, and sweat' speech on the 13th. On 15 May, Churchill signals to Roosevelt requesting the loan of old U.S. destroyers—he makes his fourth visit to France in June for discussions with the Reynaud Government, his offer of an Anglo-French Union is rejected by the French Cabinet. In July he instructs Admiral Somerville to sink the French ships at Oran unless they comply with terms. In September he makes his 'Battle of Britain' speech and presses for the formation of Commando units. October: Churchill accepts the leadership of the Conservative Party, and broadcasts an appeal to the French nation. In December he warmly welcomes the American Lend-Lease Bill.

1941 March: Churchill decides to send troops to Greece. June: He promises to aid Russia when she is attacked by Germany. In August he meets Roosevelt on board H.M.S. *Prince of Wales* in the Atlantic and they sign the Atlantic Charter.

December: Following Japan's entry into the war, Churchill visits Canada and the United States, where he addresses Congress.

1942 Churchill signs United Nations Pact in Washington (1 January). Returns to England, appoints Attlee Deputy Prime Minister, and Cripps Lord Privy Seal and Leader of the House. In March he sends Cripps to India with the offer of Dominion Status after the war. May: Churchill confers with Molotov in London. June: He goes to the United States again, where he has his first meeting with Eisenhower. On his return to England a 'No Confidence' motion is defeated in the Commons by four hundred and seventy-five votes to twenty-five, the decision is taken to occupy French North Africa and he flies to Cairo in August, giving Montgomery command of the Eighth Army and making Alexander C.-in-C. Middle East. 12 August: Churchill arrives in Moscow for his first meeting with Stalin.

1943 January: Churchill confers with Roosevelt in Casablanca, and they decide on policy of 'unconditional surrender' for the enemy. May: Churchill goes to the U.S.A. again. He receives a message from Alexander that the Tunisian Campaign is over, discusses post-war settlement and in August confers with Roosevelt at Quebec. October: After a correspondence with Stalin about Arctic convoys, he refuses to accept a note and sends Eden to Moscow. November: Churchill confers with Eisenhower and Alexander in Malta, attends Cairo Conference with Roosevelt and Chiang-Kai-Shek, meets Roosevelt and Stalin again at Teheran. In December he contracts pneumonia and convalesces at Marrakesh.

1944 January: Conference of Dominion Prime Ministers held in London. On 15 May Churchill holds the final conference before

D-Day at which the King presided. 10 June: Churchill visits the Normandy beaches. In July he visits Montgomery at his H.Q. in France and in August visits the Italian Front, has conversations with Tito in Naples and an audience with the Pope in Rome. In September he meets Roosevelt again at Quebec, then Stalin in Moscow (October) and de Gaulle in liberated Paris (November), finally flying to Athens after ordering British troops to intervene in Greece.

1945 February: Churchill attends Yalta Conference with Roosevelt and Stalin and in March he crosses the Rhine with Montgomery. 8 May: Churchill announces the end of the war in Europe in the House of Commons. 23 May: After the break-up of the Coalition Churchill forms 'Caretaker Government' until General Election. 16 July: He arrives in Berlin for the Potsdam Conference and meets Truman for the first time; agrees with him in decision to use atomic bomb against Japan. 26 July: Results of General Election declared. Conservative defeat; Churchill succeeded by Attlee as Prime Minister.

1946 Churchill receives the Order of Merit. March: In his speech at Fulton in the United States he warns against Russian ambitions and coins the expression 'iron curtain'. In September he urges the creation of a United States of Europe at Zurich, and in October announces his intention of remaining leader of the Conservative Party.

1947 Two of Churchill's paintings are accepted by the Royal Academy.

1948 April: Churchill is elected first Honorary Royal Academician Extraordinary. May: He opens the Congress of Europe at The Hague. Publication of the first volume of *The Second World War*. (Sixth and last volume published in 1954.)

1949 April: Churchill visits the United States. In June he establishes his racing stable and in August wins his first race with Colonist II.

1950 In February at Edinburgh Churchill suggests a conference with Russia, 'upon the highest level'. In the same month he is re-elected Conservative Member for Woodford.

1951 26 October: Churchill becomes Prime Minister again after the defeat of Labour in the General Election. He is also Minister of Defence. In December he sails for Washington to confer with Truman.

1952 January: Churchill visits Ottawa. March: He hands over the Ministry of Defence to Field-Marshal Alexander. December: On holiday in Jamaica he confers with Eisenhower, the United States President-elect.

1953 1 April: In anticipation of the Coronation of Queen Elizabeth II, Churchill is created Knight of the Garter. In June after suffering a slight stroke he is advised to rest by his doctor. He is awarded the Nobel Prize for Literature in October and in December attends the Bermuda Conference with Eisenhower and Laniel.

1954 June: Churchill visits Eisenhower at Washington, and signs the Potomac Charter. On 30 November he celebrates his eightieth birthday.

1955 5 April: Churchill resigns the Premiership and retires to private life. He is succeeded by Sir Anthony Eden.

1956 Churchill meets the Russian leaders, Bulganin and Kruschev, during their London visit. May–June: He visits Germany and Monaco, where he is the guest of Prince Rainier. November: In a letter to his constituents Churchill supports the British action in Suez. Publication of first two volumes of *History of the English-speaking Peoples*.

1957 Publication of third volume of *History of the English-speaking Peoples*.

1958 Sir Winston and Lady Churchill celebrate their Golden Wedding anniversary. He goes on a cruise with Mr Onassis. Publication of fourth and concluding volume of *History of the English-speaking Peoples*.

1959 Churchill visits Morocco and the United States.

LIST OF ILLUSTRATIONS

INDEX OF NAMES

*Page numbers with an asterisk indicate
an illustration*